"Wisdom That Transforms. Action That Lasts."

The Get Wisdom Commitment

At Get Wisdom Publishing we believe that true wisdom has the power to transform lives. Our mission is to equip readers with timeless insights and practical tools that inspire growth, guide decisions, and empower purposeful living. We don't just inform—we empower.

Our books combine profound understanding with real-life application, enabling readers to unlock their potential and navigate life's challenges with clarity and confidence. With each step guided by wisdom, we help you create lasting change and live the life you deserve.

When wisdom meets purpose, transformation follows.

Copyright

This book is available as an audiobook on our Amazon Jesus Follower Series page:	

Unlock Biblical Wisdom and Transform Your Faith

For more information
about the Jesus Follower Bible Study Series:
https://getwisdompublishing.com/jesus-follower-series/

Jesus Follower Bible Study Series

The WORSHIP
of a
Jesus Follower

Is Your Worship Acceptable
or in Vain?

Stephen H Berkey

GETWISDOM
PUBLISHING

This book is available as an audiobook on
our Amazon Jesus Follower Series page:

Free PDF

Living Wisely
The Life Planning Guide

A Quick-Start Guide to Purposeful Living and Wise Decisions!

Discover the five life domains: purpose, people, principles, productivity, and perspective. Wisdom is the ability to apply truth and logic to real-life decisions and produce good outcomes. It influences your choices and will produce action that lasts. Consider and apply the five practical wisdom principles for daily living. (6 pages)

Free PDF: https://getwisdompublishing.com/resource-registration/

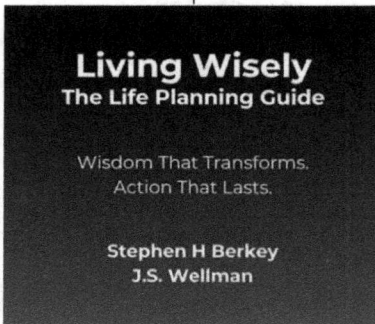

Living Wisely
The Life Planning Guide

Wisdom That Transforms.
Action That Lasts.

Stephen H Berkey
J.S. Wellman

Free PDF

Five Practical Principles For Life

When wisdom meets purpose, transformation follows.

Free PDF
Wise Decision-Making

[Get the ebook version for 99 cents]

You can make good choices.

This free resource provides a project-oriented perspective and gives ten detailed steps to analyze issues/problems to determine a solution. (26 pages)

Good decisions expand your horizons. Don't allow the fear of decision-making paralyze your ability to make good choices. Think through the reasonable alternatives and move forward. When your eyes are on the goal, making good decisions is easier.

Free PDF: https://getwisdompublishing.com/resource-registration/

Kindle ebook for 99 cents: https://www.amazon.com/dp/B09SYGWRVL/

Ebook

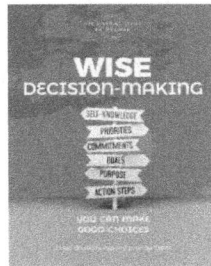

Free PDF

Make Thoughtful Decisions!

Good decisions expand your horizons.

Effective Life Change
Applying Biblical Wisdom to Live Your Best Life!

Why Read This Book?

- Transform Your life with Biblical Wisdom.
- Cultivate Practical Wisdom in Your life.
- Navigate Life with a Perspective on Biblical Truth.
- Unlock the Proverbs of the Bible to Live Your Best Life.
- Change and Transform Your life.

   Practical Application: These aren't theology or religious discussions, they're practical tools for everyday living.

Get Your Copy Today!

https://www.amazon.com/dp/1952359732
Available in Hardcover, Paperback, Kindle, and Audiobook.

The Jesus Follower Journey
Jesus Follower Bible Study Series

The Jesus Follower Bible Study Series will provide you with a complete description of the nature, characteristics, obligations, commitments, and responsibilities of a true Jesus follower.

Go to our Amazon Book Series page for your copy:
https://www.amazon.com/dp/B0DHP39P5J

The RELATIONSHIP CHARACTERISTICS of a Jesus Follower:
Are you right with God?
The ONE ANOTHER INSTRUCTIONS to a Jesus Follower:
Are you right with one another?
The WORSHIP of a Jesus Follower:
Is your worship acceptable or in vain?
The PRAYER of a Jesus Follower:
What Scripture says about unleashing the power of God.
The DANGERS of SIN for a Jesus Follower:
God HATES sin! He abhors sin!
The FOCUS for a Jesus Follower:
Keep your eyes fixed on Jesus!
The HEART Requirements of a Jesus Follower:
Follow with all your heart, mind, body, and soul!
The COMMITMENTS of a Jesus Follower:
Practical Christian living and discipleship.
The OBEDIENCE Requirements for a Jesus Follower:
Ignore at your own risk!

A related book to this series is, *Effective Life Change: Applying Biblical Wisdom to Live Your Best Life!* This book offers a practical and powerful guide to help navigate life's challenges based on the proverbial wisdom of the Bible. It offers ten commitments hat will profoundly change your life.

Table of Contents

Free PDF Wise Decision-Making...5

Effective Life Change 6

Jesus Follower Bible Study Series 7

Message From the Author..9

Introduction 12

Lesson 1 Delight in Worship...20

Lesson 2 What is Acceptable Worship? 33

Lesson 3 Old Testament Worship and the Tabernacle[1] 41

Lesson 4 the Sabbath 62

Lesson 5 God Requires a Sacrifice!...69

Lesson 6 God is Central! 83

Lesson 7 Worship in Spirit and Truth 96

Lesson 8 Worship in Heaven 113

Lesson 9 How Should We Respond? 129

Appendix A Worship Study Summary..137

Appendix B Prayer of Preparation for Worship 140

Transformation Road Map 141

Leader Guide 143

Free PDF MAKE WISE DECISIONS 158

Free PDF Life Improvement Principles 159

What Next? 160

The OBSCURE Bible Study Series 161

Life Planning Series...162

Personal Daily Prayer Guide 163

About the Author 165

Contact Us 166

Message From the Author

Dear Fellow Christ follower,

Welcome to a journey of faith and discovery.

As the author of this Bible study series, I am excited about the future because I believe this book provides the potential to transform lives, deepen our understanding of God's Word, and ignite a desire within us—a fire that draws us into the presence of our God.

Why read the Jesus Follower Series?

Deeper Roots: We all long for roots that run deep—roots anchored in truth, love, and purpose. In this series, we'll dig into the bedrock of Scripture, unearthing spiritual principles that will guide us in our faith journey.

Authentic Discipleship: Being a Jesus follower isn't about rituals or a superficial commitment. It's about walking the narrow path, picking up your cross, and living a life that loves God, follows Jesus, and loves one another. We will explore what it means to be authentic disciples.

Unveiling Mysteries: God is a source of mysteries and His Word is waiting to be discovered. Together we will examine and encounter the living Word—the One who breathes life into every syllable.

Community and Connection: We are not meant to walk this path alone. As you read, imagine joining a global community of fellow seekers. We will discuss, question, and grow together. Our shared journey will enrich us all. I encourage you to gather friends to join you in this journey.

Expected Benefits:

Renewed Passion: Prepare yourself to wake up each morning with a renewed passion for God's Word. These studies will ignite your hunger for truth and draw you into deeper relationship with the Author of Life.

Practical Application: These aren't theoretical discussions; they're practical tools for everyday living. Expect to see real-life changes—whether it's in your relationships, commitment, or prayer life.

Spiritual Resilience: Life's storms will come, but armed with the insights from God's Word, you can stand firm. Your faith will weather trials, doubts, and uncertainties. You will emerge stronger and more resilient.

Joyful Obedience: As we explore the nature of discipleship, you'll discover that obedience isn't a burden—it's a joy. The path of obedience leads to peace, and you'll find yourself saying, "Yes, Lord!" with newfound delight.

Let's Begin!

So, turn the page. Dive into the first chapter. Let the words seep into your soul. And remember, you're not alone—we're on this pilgrimage together. May these books be more than ink on paper; may they be stepping stones toward a life that leads to eternity. Amen!

"We believe applied wisdom empowers life change. Our books provide clarity, inspiration, and tools to equip readers to live their best life."

My prayer is that you will

Be tenacious like Job
Walk like Enoch
Believe like Abraham
Wrestle like Jacob
Dress like Joseph
Lead like Moses
Conquer like Deborah
Be fearless like Shamgar
Inspire like Josuha
Influence like Esther
Dance like David
Ask like Jabez
Have the faith of Daniel
Pray like Elijah
Trust like Elisha
Commit like Isaiah
Be courageous like Benaiah
Rebuild like Nehemiah
Be obedient like Hosea
Be zealous like Zacchaeus
Surrender like Mary
Stand firm like Stephen
Speak like Peter
Seize opportunities like Philip
Submit like Paul
Overcome like the Elect (Saints)
Worship like the 24 Elders
and
Love like Jesus

Steve

Introduction

Book Description

Unlock the transformative power of true worship with this bible study. "*The WORSHIP of a Jesus Follower*" is an eye-opening exploration that will revolutionize your understanding of what it means to worship God.

Are you confident that your worship is pleasing to God? This thought-provoking study delves deep into Scripture to reveal the essence of authentic worship, challenging common misconceptions, and inspiring a renewed passion for connecting with God.

You will discover:

• The surprising truth about what makes worship acceptable or vain in God's eyes.

• Ancient wisdom from Old Testament practices and their relevance today.

• The critical link between sacrifice and genuine worship.

• How to worship "in spirit and truth."

• A glimpse into the awe-inspiring worship occurring in Heaven.

From the Tabernacle to modern-day churches, this comprehensive study traces the evolution of worship while uncovering timeless principles that will transform your spiritual life. You'll gain fresh insights into topics like:

- The significance of the Sabbath in worship.
- Why God must be central in our adoration.
- The eternal nature of worship and its implications for believers.

Perfect for individual study or small group discussions, each chapter concludes with thought-provoking questions and practical applications to deepen your worship experience.

Don't settle for routine religious practices – embark on a journey to discover worship that truly honors God and changes lives. Whether you're a seasoned believer or new to faith, this study will ignite a fresh fire of devotion in your heart.

We Reap What We Sow!

In a number of his proverbs, King Solomon suggests that doing what is right is to be preferred over evil. King Solomon was known world-wide for his great wisdom. He wrote and recorded many proverbs recognized for their practical insight and wisdom. He describes the nature of righteousness as being immovable and that it will stand above evil.

Is your desire for doing what is "right" rooted deeply or is it planted in shallow soil that can easily be washed away? Solomon indicated that the wicked would ultimately be overthrown and that the righteous would survive because their character had roots that were deep and impossible to dislodge.

Solomon argued that it was better to be on the side of the righteous. The reasoning is the same as the man who builds his house, business, or life on rock versus sand. If we build on sand (questionable ways) then our hopes and plans will never stand up against the storms of life. If we build on rock (character, commitment, and obedience) our plans will hold firm.

We do reap what we sow and if we sow badly because we have rejected what is right, the wise counsel of friends, or our core values, we will reap the negative consequences. Those who think they know everything frequently reject wisdom and follow their own plans and schemes. It has been said that those who insist on following their own foolish ways will often end up choking on them.

> *Choices produce consequences*
> *which direct the course of life.*
> *Consequences shape lives.*
> *Therefore, count the cost!*

INTRODUCTION TO WORSHIP

The following is an overview of the worship material in this study. It highlights some of the more important issues that we will cover in detail beginning in Lesson 1. We will examine what God requires. You may not realize that your worship can be unacceptable to God. That may raise the question of how important worship should be in your life. You may be concerned that you don't really "feel" worship! So, what is worship? Let's start with the definition.

Definition

"Worship" is encountering the living God. The object of our worship is God. Worship tends to mean different things to different people but for this study when we refer to worship it will mean:

> *Worship is the ceremony or response we invoke to express*
> *our devotion, allegiance, and honor to God. It can be by*
> *direct acknowledgement of His presence, nature, ways, or*
> *claims; and it can be both inward (love, joy, trust*
> *adoration) or outward expressions: service, prayer, praise,*
> *singing, dance, giving . . .*

The Importance of Worship

> **Psalm 1:1-3** *Blessed is the man who does not walk in the counsel of the wicked or stand in the way of sinners or sit in the seat of mockers. 2 But his <u>delight</u> is in the law of the Lord, and on his law he meditates day and night. 3 He is like a tree planted by streams of water, which yields its fruit in season and whose leaf does not wither. Whatever he does prospers.* NIV

Delight in the Lord is another great way to describe the nature of worship. It is the committed attitude of the true worshipper who says, "O that I might worship you, my Lord and my Redeemer!" It is in the joy of one who shouts or sings, *"The Lord reigns; let the earth rejoice; let the many coastlands be glad!"* (Psalm 97:1)

WHAT GOD REQUIRES

> ***Love the Lord your God with all your heart and with all your soul and with all your mind.***
> Matthew 22:37

Genesis 22:1-18 *Sometime later God <u>tested</u> Abraham. He said to him, "Abraham!" "Here I am," he replied. 2 Then God said, "Take your son, your only son, Isaac, whom you love, and go to the region of Moriah. Sacrifice him there as a burnt offering on one of the mountains I will tell you about." 3 Early the next morning Abraham got up and saddled his donkey. . . . On the third day Abraham looked up and saw the place in the distance. 5 He said to his servants, "Stay here with the donkey while I and the boy go over there. We will worship and then we will come back to you." . . . 12 "Do not lay a hand on the boy," he said. "Do not do anything to him. Now I know that you fear God, because you have not withheld from me your son, your only son." . . . 18 and through your offspring all nations on earth will be blessed, because you have obeyed me."* NIV

In Genesis 22:18 God says that Abraham will be a blessing to the nations because he <u>obeyed</u> God's voice. We should note that God provided the substitute (ram) for Isaac. Man is destined to die for his sins, but Jesus (God) died in our place, just as He provided the ram as a substitute sacrifice for Isaac. Abraham worshiped God by (1) fearing Him, (2) obeying Him, and (3) not withholding something very precious from Him.

WHAT WORSHIP MUST WE AVOID?

In John 4:22 we learn that the Samaritans were worshipping what they did not know. Their worship was wrong and might be considered ignorant. In Romans 1:22-23 the worship is also improper because they were worshipping idols (birds, animals, and reptiles). The people were described as fools. They reduced God to a man-made image.

Israel did the same in the Old Testament. Idols plagued them from the day they tried to take the Promised Land and disobeyed God by not destroying the sinful residents and their gods. Israel even brought inferior sacrifices to worship when God had specified they were to bring the best:

> **Malachi 1:8** *When you offer blind animals in sacrifice, is that not evil? And when you offer those that are lame or sick, is that not evil? Present that to your governor; will he accept you or show you favor? says the Lord of hosts.* ESV

Their worship had no real value. It was marked by futility, it was inferior, and it lacked real devotion to God.

In Matthew 15:9 Jesus says that the people worshipped in vain because they were following the rules of men rather that the commandments of God. We will dig deeper into acceptable worship in Lesson 3 where we will learn what is required for acceptable worship. It is clear that our worship must be acceptable to God.

> **Leviticus 1:3** *"If his offering is a burnt offering from the herd, he shall offer a male without blemish. He shall bring it*

*to the entrance of the tent of meeting, that he may be
<u>accepted</u> before the Lord."* ESV

Hebrews 12:28-29 *Therefore let us be grateful for receiving
a kingdom that cannot be shaken, and thus let us offer to
God <u>acceptable</u> worship, with reverence and awe, 29 for our
God is a consuming fire.* ESV

KEY REQUIREMENTS IN OLD AND NEW TESTAMENTS

<u>OLD TESTAMENT (NIV):</u>

> **Exodus 20:3** *You shall have <u>no other gods</u> before me.*

> **2 Kings 17:*36*** *But the LORD . . . is the one you must <u>worship</u>.*

> **Psalms 95:6** *Come, let us <u>bow down in worship</u>, let us <u>kneel</u>
> before the LORD our Maker.*

> **1 Chronicles 16:29** *. . . worship the LORD in the splendor of
> <u>his holiness</u>.*

<u>NEW TESTAMENT (NIV):</u>

> **Matthew 22:37** *. . . Love the Lord your God with <u>all your
> heart</u> and with <u>all your soul</u> and with <u>all your mind</u>.*

> **Hebrews 9:19-22** *Therefore, brothers, since we have
> confidence to enter the Most Holy Place by the blood of
> Jesus, 20 by a new and living way opened for us through the
> curtain, that is, his body, 21 and since we have a great priest
> over the house of God, 22 let us <u>draw near to God</u> with a
> <u>sincere heart</u> in full assurance of faith, having our <u>hearts
> sprinkled to cleanse us</u> from a guilty conscience and having
> our <u>bodies washed with pure water</u>.*

This study is a serious look at what God's Word says is required
for acceptable worship. We will examine both our personal and
corporate worship. There may be questions that make you

uncomfortable. If they offend anyone – that is not the intent. The hope is that we look closely and truthfully at our worship with the intent of making changes to both our personal and corporate worship where that is appropriate.

If this is the first time you have seriously studied the subject of worship, be prepared to learn things you did not know, you may even be surprised or even a bit shocked at what the Bible has to say about worship. Enjoy the adventure.

OUR PRAYER

Lord, I pray for a new and revived passion for worship in my life, for Your presence to manifest itself in my worship. Lord Jesus, I want a seeking heart and a deep desire to know You in worship. Make Yourself known to me and give me an acute sensitivity to the Spirit during times of worship.

Father, cleanse my heart, mind, and spirit, so that sin cannot interfere with my worship – I want to openly express my love, adoration, and praise for Your greatness. I want an all-consuming hunger to know You in worship. Please eliminate distractions so that I can concentrate only on You. Father, give me a new fervency for Christ during worship.

I pray that all I do and say in worship will glorify and exalt your Name. That you will be high and lifted up, that Your Name will be magnified and glorified above all things great and small.

I ask that your majesty and splendor be revealed to me. Help me to truly know the living God. I want to be stunned by Your greatness. Great is the Lord and greatly to be praised; He is to be feared above all gods! (Psalm 96:4) May I be overwhelmed by the majesty of Your awesome faithfulness and convinced of Your grace. I pray that I would humbly seek the heart of God. You O Lord are the one true God: Father, Son, and Holy Spirit. Halleluiah! Amen.

Group Discussion or Individual Study

These studies can be done individually or in a small discussion group. An important value of the study is in the discussion questions. We all see life differently and the thoughts and ideas shared in a group will often lead to a richer understanding of the Scripture. We recommend doing these studies in a group, if possible.

Format of Lessons

The format of the lessons is not the same in each book. We chose a format that best fit the material.

WHAT DO I WANT TO REMEMBER?

Enter some notes and information that you want to remember about this lesson. It might be a Scripture verse or two, something new you learned, something you want to do, something you want to change, or just something you want to be sure to remember.

Focused Biblical Wisdom.
Everyday Faith Application!

Lesson 1
Delight in Worship

MEDITATION

Meditate on the following Scripture during your Quiet Time this week:

Hebrews 10:18-22 *Therefore, brothers, since we have confidence to enter the Most Holy Place by the blood of Jesus, 20 by a new and living way opened for us through the curtain, that is, his body, 21 and since we have a great priest over the house of God, 22 let us draw near to God with a sincere heart in full assurance of faith, having our hearts sprinkled to cleanse us from a guilty conscience and having our bodies washed with pure water.* NIV

Related subjects that might be considered for your meditation:

- The Most Holy Place: the presence of God.
- The blood of Jesus: the necessity of a blood sacrifice – life is in the blood.
- Through the curtain: the separation between man and God (now removed).
- The great priest: Jesus.
- Hearts sprinkled to cleanse us: Jesus' blood covers our sin.
- Our bodies washed with pure water: we are clean.

NOTES:

INTRODUCTION

Before we begin the more serious subjects associated with worship, let's begin with "delight." This term might be one of the better descriptions of what it means to worship God.

Delight is a caring for or an affinity for something that is generated from the heart. The psalmist illustrates this feeling when he says:

> **Psalm 40:8-9** *I desire to do your will, O my God; your law is within my heart." 9 I proclaim righteousness in the great assembly; I do not seal my lips, as you know, O Lord.* NIV

Delight might also be described as *intimate worship*. It means I earnestly seek out the Lord and celebrate the majesty of His Name! When I delight in the Lord I am engaging in heartfelt worship. This feeling or activity is not being generated from the mind but from the heart – the place of inner truth.

We are instructed to delight in a number of things throughout Scripture. For example we are to:

Delight in the law (Psalm 1:2).
Delight in the Almighty (Job 22:26).
Delight in His deliverance (Psalm 35:9).
Delight in the Lord (Psalm 37:4).
Delight in understanding (Proverbs 18:2).
Delight in the nearness of God (Isaiah 58:2).
Delight in the knowledge of God (Jeremiah 9:24).
Delight in love, justice, righteousness (Jeremiah 9:24).
Delight in the Son; listen to Him (Matthew 17:5).

The word *delight* and its derivatives occur over 110 times in the Bible, while the word *worship* occurs about 200 times. Delight is directed toward God and occurs almost exclusively in the Old Testament.

SHE LOVED MUCH

Luke 7:36-38 *Now one of the Pharisees invited Jesus to have dinner with him, so he went to the Pharisee's house and reclined at the table. 37 When a woman who had lived a sinful life in that town learned that Jesus was eating at the Pharisee's house, she brought an alabaster jar of perfume, 38 and as she stood behind him at his feet weeping, she began to wet his feet with her tears. Then she wiped them with her hair, kissed them and poured perfume on them.* NIV

Maybe you had to be there to have the full impact of this act touch your heart. This passage describes the dedication of someone totally in touch with the object of her worship – Christ Jesus. She was not ashamed of her actions. She was not afraid to show the emotion that characterized her relationship with her Savior. The perfume was very valuable and yet she poured it all out on Jesus' feet. Some might suggest this act was a great waste while others consider it a dramatic act of worship.

The woman did several gracious and loving acts at Jesus' feet: weeping, anointing Him with oil, kissing His feet, and wiping His feet with her hair. Why? The only hint we have of a motive is Jesus' comment after He told the Pharisee the parable: "That's why she loved much." Jesus related this love to being forgiven. Therefore, one explanation for her actions is that they were done out of love because she had been forgiven much. She was extremely grateful and showed her love through her worship.

Her tears would seem to be those of joy and gladness for the release she must have felt knowing that she was forgiven for the lifestyle she had been living. The point of the parable Jesus told was that someone who has been forgiven much responds with great love and gratitude, while someone who has been forgiven less will respond with less. This woman realized she was a sinner and needed forgiveness to be right with God. She expressed her great love toward Jesus through these acts of worship because she had been forgiven much.

But why was she in the Pharisee's house doing all this? After realizing the great burden that had been lifted from her shoulders and hearing that Jesus was nearby in the home of one of the Pharisees, she must have wanted to demonstrate her great love and gratitude. What could she do? The perfume was the profit from her trade and probably represented in some way her life as a "sinful woman." What a better act of gratitude and release than to dispose of it by anointing Jesus' feet? The woman used her most treasured possession (the perfume) to proclaim her commitment of faith. Words were unnecessary! Through the use of the perfume and the wiping of His feet with her hair she was surrendering to Him.

What would you have done? Would you have openly and aggressively gained entrance and then shamelessly demonstrated your love? Or would you be worried about what people would say or think?

The perfume may have been the only valuable thing the woman owned. It likely represented:

- her most valuable possession and she gave it to Jesus.
- an offering of her life (past and future) to her King.
- her saying, "I care only about my identity in Christ."
- a very personal, humble, and public act of love.
- an extravagant expression of faith.

One might suggest that this act of worship was a bit over-the-top. Or we might be overwhelmed by the authenticity of the woman. This may have been a Damascus Road type of experience – she was simply so overcome by being in the presence of Jesus and her emotions spilled out in His presence.

This story certainly raises some personal questions:

1. What do you love most? What is your most treasured possession? Do you love Jesus more than your most treasured possession? Would you give up your most treasured possession for Him?

2. This woman was overwhelmed with gratitude. She was sold-out to Christ. What would have to happen in your life today in order for you to give your savings (or most of it) to a Kingdom cause?

3. Do your actions speak for you? Would your actions convict you of being delighted in Jesus?

4. Do you need to do something bold for Christ?

5. Do you need to imitate this woman in any way?

THE 24 ELDERS

Revelation 4:10-11; 19:4 *the twenty-four elders fall down before him who sits on the throne, and worship him who lives for ever and ever. They lay their crowns before the throne and say: 11 "You are worthy, our Lord and God, to receive glory and honor and power, for you created all things, and by your will they were created and have their being." . . . 19:4 The twenty-four elders and the four living creatures fell down and worshiped God, who was seated on the throne. And they cried: "Amen, Hallelujah!"* NIV

I want to worship and delight in the Lord like the 24 elders. I want to unashamedly lay anything of value at His feet. I want to approach Him in submission and humility like these elders who were sold-out to their King. This is an act of worship, just like the woman in the story with Jesus.

Remember, we defined worship in the Introduction as:

> *The ceremony or response we invoke to express*
> *our devotion, allegiance, and honor to God.*
> *It can be the direct acknowledgment of His presence,*
> *nature, ways, or claims; it can be both inward*
> *(love, joy, trust . . .) or it can be outward expressions*
> *like service, prayer, posture, praise, singing, giving . . .*

In Revelation 4:11 the 24 elders tell us why they worship: because He is worthy! They also confirm that their worship is because He is the creator and sustainer of all things. Worship is a function that will never end because God is eternal and has no end. Evangelism will ultimately cease when eternity begins but the worship of the Godhead will be eternal. Therefore, if there is one practice we want to get right while we are still here on earth practicing for eternity, it should be that we worship in spirit and in truth and not in vain. Worship that is unacceptable to God should be eliminated from our life.

Why would the 24 elders throw their crowns on the floor? There are various reasons why this might occur, but it seems obvious that they recognize they only have the crowns because of Him. They have crowns because of the power of God in their lives and only God Himself is really worthy to wear a crown – it is an act of submission and worship. They are acknowledging God as totally worthy and deserving of their adoration. He has earned all their praise and worship.

The most critical aspect of worship is determining and knowing who we worship. The what, where, and when have very little importance compared to the who!

> **Mark 12:29-30** . . . *Hear, O Israel, the Lord our God, the Lord is one. 30 Love the Lord your God with all your heart and with all your soul and with all your mind and with all your strength.* NIV

Worship focused on God should be at the top of our priority list. It is the natural result of loving God with all our heart, mind, body, and soul!

This raises some important questions for each of us:

1. AM I PREPARED: Do I come to worship prepared (clean hands and a pure heart)?
Who may ascend the hill of the Lord? Who may stand in his holy place? 4 He who has clean hands and a pure heart, who does not lift up his soul to an idol or swear by what is false. Psalms 24:3-4 NIV

2. IS MY HEART RIGHT: Am I coming to worship with the right heart attitude?
Do I come to worship humble and with a contrite heart (surrendered and submissive)?

3. AM I FOCUSED: Is the Lord Jesus my primary focus, and the number one priority of my life?
Is Jesus constantly before me? Is He foremost in my thoughts? Is my life God-centered?

4. AM I A LIVING SACRIFICE: Is my life a living sacrifice onto God? (Romans 12:1)
I appeal to you therefore, brothers, by the mercies of God, to present your bodies as a living sacrifice, holy and acceptable to God, which is your spiritual worship. ESV

Have I submitted my life to Christ? Have I laid my crowns at His feet like the 24 elders?

TEN LEPERS

Luke 17:11-19   *Now on his way to Jerusalem, Jesus traveled along the border between Samaria and Galilee. 12 As he was going into a village, ten men who had leprosy met him. They stood at a distance 13 and called out in a loud voice, "Jesus, Master, have pity on us!" 14 When he saw them, he said, "Go, show yourselves to the priests." And as they went, they were cleansed. 15 One of them, when he saw he was healed, came back, praising God in a loud voice. 16 He threw himself at Jesus' feet and thanked him — and he was a Samaritan. 17 Jesus asked, "Were not all ten cleansed? Where are the other nine? 18 Was no one found to return and give praise to God except this foreigner?" 19 Then he said to him, "Rise and go; your faith has made you well."* NIV

To me, this is one of the saddest stories in the New Testament. Where are the other nine lepers who were healed? Obviously Jesus thinks they should have returned because He asks, "Were not all ten cleansed?" Oh, that I never become so hardened and ungrateful that I do not thank my God for what He does for me!

A leper in those days was unloved, unwanted, and treated as an outcast. He likely wanted to die and was both emotionally and mentally damaged. He was not able to touch and hold children or grandchildren. Lepers had good reason to cry out, "Why me, Lord?"

Therefore, if you were a leper and were healed in a miraculous way, how would you feel? What would you do? Biblical history tells us this was not the only time a very high degree of ingratitude was on display. For example, the Israelites began worshipping a golden calf within weeks of escaping Egypt, and they grumbled about the free manna and quail.

What do you think spawns ingratitude? It may be some of the following:

1. Not working for the things you get – free things are usually worth what you pay for them.

2. Feelings of superiority; being spoiled and having everything given to you.

3. Being rich and having all the physical things you want and desire.

4. Feelings of entitlement.

5. Being self-absorbed; being totally focused on self.

The Bible says to examine ourselves (2 Corinthians 13:5). We are to test ourselves when necessary and act like people of faith. Do you need to thank someone? What are you personally thankful to God for? How might you show or demonstrate gratitude to God?

There are a number of significant benefits that the Lord has provided to us (other than life, health, and salvation). For example: (1) spouse, children, and grandchildren; (2) spiritual gifts and skills; (3) intelligence; (4) daily provision; (5) protection; and (6) the Holy Spirit.

Every one of us can thank God for something, including these things!

DELIGHT YOURSELF

John Piper says, "For God is most reflected in me when I am most delighted in Him." How do I delight in the Lord? What does that mean? How do I get both my heart and mind aligned on delighting? In Psalm 37:4 we have the command to delight in Him and a promise that ought to motivate us to worship:

> Delight yourself in the Lord and he will <u>give you the desires of your heart.</u> NIV

Delight means we are highly pleased, elated, overjoyed, happy, or thrilled. If something is to be "reflected in me" then it must be made manifest (it must be seen in me), have some influence on me, or be mirrored in my words or actions. I might show or display it outwardly. I must reflect my delight! That delight must be real heart-felt feelings for my God. There can be no competing delights.

Based on the following Scriptures, why are we to delight?

Psalm 37:4 _____
Psalm 35:9 _____
Psalm 112:1 _____
Isaiah 11:3 _____
Isaiah 58:13 _____
Isaiah 61:10 _____
Isaiah 58:2 _____
James 4:8 _____

Delighting yourself in the Lord should involve doing what is pleasing to Him. What do the following suggest God delights in?

Romans 12:1-2 _____
Romans 14:17-18 _____
Philippians 4:18 _____
1 Timothy 5:4 _____
Hebrews 13:29-21 _____

DISCUSSION QUESTIONS

Q1. How do you react to the above discussion on worship?

Q2. In 50 words or less describe the act of worship. What does it mean for <u>you</u> to worship? (Describe your personal thoughts – not some textbook answer.)

Q3. Excluding the physical act of bowing down, what attitude of worship is being demonstrated in the following:

> **Exodus 34:8** *Moses bowed to the ground at once and worshiped.*
> **Ruth 2:10** *At this, she bowed down with her face to the ground. . . .*
> **Isaiah 44:17** *From the rest he makes a god, his idol; he bows down to it and worships. He prays to it and says, "Save me; you are my god."*

Q4. For <u>you</u>, what is the most important issue regarding the subject of worship? Explain.

Much of the controversy surrounding worship today would be resolved if we would remember that God alone is God. He is the God revealed in the Bible. He has not changed. He is holy! He is King! He is majestic. He is the one who will return riding the white horse. And His standards have not changed. Thus, the fundamental issue is not <u>how</u> we worship, but <u>who</u> we worship.

Q5. Is it appropriate to be politically correct and agree that everyone is free to worship God in his own way? Why? Why not?

Q6. Relate Psalm 24:3-4 to worship.
Psalms 24:3-4 Who shall ascend the hill of the Lord? And who shall stand in his holy place? 4 He who has clean hands and a pure heart, who does not lift up his soul to what is false and does not swear deceitfully. ESV

24:3. What does it mean to "ascend the hill?" Where are they going?

24:4. How are they supposed to come?

Q7. Who is God? Who is it that you worship?
In the following space or on a separate page describe your God, in enough detail that someone relatively unfamiliar with God would have a reasonable understanding of who you are describing. Maximum 100 words. [Your Group Leader may ask several people to share their descriptions.]

Are you happy with your description? Did you need more or fewer words? What would have to change in order for you to provide a better description?

Q8. What is the best way (means) we have to know God?

Q9. Read Revelation 5

9a. In Revelation 5 the one who could open the scroll is described using three different names that identify who He is. What are those names and what do they signify?

(1)

(2)

(3)

9b. Who praises God in Revelation 5:13?

It can be said that being overwhelmed by the greatness of God begins in the mind but does not end until it reaches the heart. Touching the mind is relatively easy, but what allows it to travel from the mind to the heart?

Q10. What have you personally learned about worship?

a. What is the most important thing you learned?

b. What was new?

c. What don't you understand or what remains fuzzy or confusing?

WHAT DO I WANT TO REMEMBER?

Enter some notes and information that you want to remember about this lesson. It might be a Scripture verse or two, something new you learned, something you want to do, something you want to change, or just something you want to be sure to remember.

Wisdom to Action
Challenge

Reflect on your daily routine. What one change can you make this week to prioritize your delight in God and express it through authentic worship?

Lesson 2
What is Acceptable Worship?

INTRODUCTION

How or why does authentic worship occur? What happens in true worship? John Piper says that the affections or pleasure or maybe even joy that results in magnifying God must come from truly understanding His glory. So Piper suggests that if worship is dry and unsatisfying, it may be because there is a famine of the Word of God.

The only devotion that honors God is that which is solidly rooted in Biblical truth. Religious feelings or responses that do not come from a true understanding of God are not holy, no matter how intense. You can wave your hands all you want, but if you do not know God and understand what you are doing and why are you doing it. Rote and emotional responses in worship can be unacceptable to God unless the motivation is true heartfelt devotion.

In this lesson we are going to focus on what is acceptable worship. What does God say is acceptable and what is unacceptable? Remember, we have defined worship as:

> *Worship is the ceremony or response we invoke to express our devotion, allegiance, and honor to God. It can be the direct acknowledgement of His presence, nature, ways, or claims. Worship can be both inward (love, joy, trust, adoration, etc.) or it can be expressed in our outward expressions (service, prayer, posture, praise, singing, dancing, giving, etc.).*

Q1. Based on the following passages, what are the requirements for acceptable worship? Fill in the blanks from the verses that follow:

1. We must do it (worship) _____.
Leviticus 1:3-4 *If his offering is a burnt offering from the herd, he shall offer a male without blemish. He shall bring it to the entrance of the tent of meeting, that he may be <u>accepted</u> before the Lord.* ESV
Hebrews 12:28-29 *Therefore let us be grateful for receiving a kingdom that cannot be shaken, and thus let us offer to God <u>acceptable</u> worship, with reverence and awe, 29 for our God is a consuming fire.* ESV

2. No _____ is required. We are the _____ and can approach God directly.
1 Peter 2:9 But you are a chosen people, a royal <u>priesthood</u>, a holy nation, . . .

3. We must come to worship God with or through _____.
John 10:9 *I am the door. If anyone enters by me, he will be saved . . .* ESV
John 14:6 *I am the way, and the truth, and the life. No one comes to the Father except through me.* ESV

4. The first thing I must do in approaching a holy God is to be free of _____ .
Leviticus 9:7 *Moses said to Aaron, "Come to the altar and sacrifice your <u>sin offering</u> and your burnt offering and make atonement for yourself and the people . . .* NIV

5. Like the Old Testament priest, I must approach God in worship with _____ and_____.
Psalms 24:3-4 *Who shall ascend the hill of the Lord? And who shall stand in his holy place? 4 He who has clean hands and a pure heart, . . .* ESV

6. My entire _____ is an act of worship.
Romans 12:1 *Therefore, I urge you, brothers, in view of God's mercy, to offer your bodies as living sacrifices . . .* NIV

7. Just as the priest was an intermediary between man and God, we too must bring the message of _____ and _____ to me.

John 8:12 *When Jesus spoke again to the people, he said, "I am the light of the world. Whoever follows me will never walk in darkness, but will have the light of life." NIV*

8. Our worship must be rooted in the _____.

Leviticus 24:8-9 *This bread is to be set out before the LORD regularly, Sabbath after Sabbath, on behalf of the Israelites, as a lasting covenant. 9 It belongs to Aaron and his sons, who are to eat it in a holy place . . . NIV*

John 6:35 *Then Jesus declared, "I am the bread of life. He who comes to me will never go hungry, and he who believes in me will never be thirsty." NIV*

9. Our worship is a matter of the _____.

Mark 12:30 *Love the Lord your God with all your heart and with all your soul and with all your mind and with all your strength.' NIV*

Romans 10:9-10 *That if you confess with your mouth, "Jesus is Lord," and believe in your heart that God raised him from the dead, you will be saved. 10 For it is with your heart that you believe and are justified, and it is with your mouth that you confess and are saved. NIV*

10. We must come to worship in an attitude of _____.

Revelation 8:3-4 *Another angel, who had a golden censer, came and stood at the altar. He was given much incense to offer, with the prayers of all the saints, on the golden altar before the throne. 4 The smoke of the incense, together with the prayers of the saints, went up before God from the angel's hand. NIV*

We must understand that our worship can be underlined unacceptable to God if it is:

- Ignorant - know not what we do (John 4:22).
- improper - idolatrous (Romans 1:22-23).
- inferior - God wants only our best (Malachi 1:8).
- in vain - following the rules of men (Matthew 15:9).

How does authentic worship occur? True worship must include inward feelings that reflect our gratitude and joy for the love, grace, patience, and trustworthiness of God. Hypocritical worship is going through the motions (singing, praying, reciting, giving, dancing, etc.) which outwardly indicate affections that do not really exist. Worship that is acceptable is:

> *"Where people are not stunned by the greatness of God, how can they be sent with the ringing message, 'Great is the Lord and greatly to be praised; he is to be feared above all Gods!'" (Ps 96:4) Savoring the vision of a triumphant God in worship precedes spreading it to others. All of history is moving toward one great goal, the worship of God among the peoples of the earth. The great sin of the world is that we have failed to delight in God so to reflect His glory. For God is most reflected in us when we are most delighted in Him."* John Piper[2]

WORSHIP RESPONSES

What types of responses in worship are authentic?

Perhaps the first response of the heart from seeing the majestic holiness of God is _stunned silence_ (Psalm 46:10). Stunned silence can produce a sense of _awe, wonder, and reverence_ at the sheer magnitude of God (Psalm 33:8). A holy fear of God's righteous power should overcome us (Isaiah 8:13; Psalm 5:7). This "holy fear" can result in _brokenness and contrition_ for our ungodly acts (Psalm 51:7). Out of this feeling of brokenness there may arise a deep _longing for God_ (Psalm 42:1-2; Psalm 63:1; Psalm 73:25-26).

In authentic worship we long to experience God Himself, to see Him (like Moses), to know Him, or be in His presence. Thus we experience pleasure, joy, and delight.

> **Psalms 16:11** *You make known to me the path of life; in your presence there is fullness of joy; at your right hand are pleasures forevermore.* ESV

It would seem that without the engagement of the heart, we do not truly worship. This engagement produces feelings, emotions, and affections. John Piper says, "Where feelings for God are dead, worship is dead." True worship must include inward feelings that reflect our gratitude and joy for the love, grace, patience, and trustworthiness of God.

Unauthentic worship is going through the motions (singing, praying, reciting, giving, dancing, etc.) which outwardly indicate devotion that does not really exist.

> **Matthew 15:7-9** *You hypocrites! Isaiah was right when he prophesied about you: 8 "These people honor me with their lips, but their hearts are far from me. 9 They worship me in vain; their teachings are but rules taught by men."* NIV

If God's truth is displayed to us from His Word or from His creation, and we do not feel longing, hope, or awe, then we may sing, gesture, and give all we want, but it will not be real and authentic worship. Worship reflects back to God the joy that resides within us. It can be true worship only when affections come from the heart.

Q2. How would <u>you</u> describe the heart we are examining in this Lesson?

The "heart" is important because:

Matt 22:37 Jesus replied: Love the Lord your God with all <u>your heart</u>.
Matt 6:21 For where your treasure is, there <u>your heart</u> will be also.
Rom 10:10 For it is with <u>your heart</u> that you believe and are justified.
Eph 5:19 Sing and make music in <u>your heart</u> to the Lord.
Col 3:23 Whatever you do, work at it with all <u>your heart</u>.

In the Bible the word "heart" has a much broader meaning than it does today. Nearly all the references to the heart in the Bible refer to some aspect of human personality. The Bible describes purity, evil, sincerity, and rebelliousness relative to the heart of man. The heart is that which is thought of as being central to or the core of man.

God knows the heart of each person (1 Samuel 16:7). Since a person speaks and acts from his heart, he is to guard it well (Proverbs 4:23; Matthew 15:18-19). As we have seen above the most important duty of man is to love God with the whole heart (Matthew 22:37). Thus man believes in Christ and experiences a relationship with God that resides in the heart.

HEART

According to Scripture the heart the inner being of man and it is the source of good and evil deeds, lust, and passion as well as the dwelling place of the Divine (Ephesians 3:17).

What is done by man is often described as being done by an obedient heart (Romans 6:17). The heart is the source of worship.

WHAT DOES IT MEAN TO WORSHIP?

"Worship is the missing jewel of the church. God's people need to recapture the meaning of worship and develop a vision for all of life as a sacrificial act of worship." A. W. Tozer

Man's problem is sin:

Genesis 4:6-7 *The Lord said to Cain, "Why are you angry, and why has your face fallen? 7 If you do well, will you not be accepted? And if you do not do well, <u>sin is crouching at the door</u>. Its desire is for you, but you must rule over it."* ESV

> **NOTE: It is important to understand the progression of the sin sacrifice concept in the Bible?**
> - A lamb for a man (Genesis 4:4 – Abel)
> - A lamb for a family (Exodus 12:3-5 – Jewish slaves)
> - A lamb for a nation (Leviticus 16:34 – Israel)
> - A lamb for the world (John 1:29 – All)

God's provision is His Son:
1 Peter 1:18-19 *knowing that you were ransomed from the futile ways inherited from your forefathers, not with perishable things such as silver or gold, 19 but <u>with the precious blood of Christ</u>, like that of a lamb without blemish or spot.* ESV

God's answer is the living stones, a holy priesthood:
1 Peter 2:5 *you yourselves like living stones are being built up as a <u>spiritual house</u>, to be a <u>holy priesthood</u>, to offer spiritual sacrifices acceptable to God through Jesus Christ.* ESV

DISCUSSION QUESTIONS

1. If a friend asked you what it means to worship, what would you say?

2. If that same friend asked, "What is the most important thing I should do in worship?" How would you answer?

3. Why do Christian congregations sing? Is that a requirement in the Bible?

4. How important is having your heart engaged during a worship service? Why?

5. What kind of response do you think is appropriate, expected, or desired in a worship service? Why?

THE NEXT LESSON

We have discussed many of the issues and concepts of worship. Now we are going to step back and examine worship in the Old Testament and in particular the importance and meaning of the Tabernacle. Most of us know little about the importance of the Tabernacle and its meaning. We pray that this will provide a rich understanding of God and Old Testament worship.

WHAT DO I WANT TO REMEMBER?

Enter some notes and information that you want to remember about this lesson. It might be a Scripture verse or two, something new you learned, something you want to do, something you want to change, or just something you want to be sure to remember.

Wisdom to Action
Challenge

How can you intentionally engage with God's Word this week to transform your heart and fuel more genuine worship? Choose a specific passage to study and apply.

Lesson 3
Old Testament Worship and the Tabernacle[1]

INTRODUCTION

"Worship" is the Hebrew word "*shachah*" which means to prostrate oneself or bow down. In the Old Testament it is the common term for coming before God to honor Him. The word "worship" appears first in Genesis 22, in the story of Abraham where God commanded Abraham to sacrifice his son Isaac as a burnt offering. A "burnt offering" is described in Leviticus 1 and is defined as a voluntary offering by fire that is a soothing aroma to the Lord. When the person making the sacrifice lays his hand on the head of the burnt offering (sacrifice), it was intended to make atonement for sins. Atonement is the act by which God restores the relationship of harmony and unity between Himself and His people.

In Genesis 22:18 God says that Abraham will be a blessing to the nations because he <u>obeyed</u> God's voice. Remember God provided the substitute sacrifice for Isaac. Man is destined to die for his sins, but Jesus (God) is our substitute sacrifice.

SECTION 1 – The Tabernacle

On Mount Sinai, after the Lord had given the commandments, judgments, and ordinances to Moses, He instructed Moses to construct a tabernacle. This was to be a center for worship and a place where the people could focus upon the presence of the Lord. It would be the very dwelling place of God. It's clear that God desires an intimate relationship because He desires the worship of His people. No other faith has a God who wants to be near and dwell in the presence of His followers.

How do we worship a God like this? God gave specific instructions on how the Jewish people were to approach Him and how the tabernacle, where He would "reside," should be built.

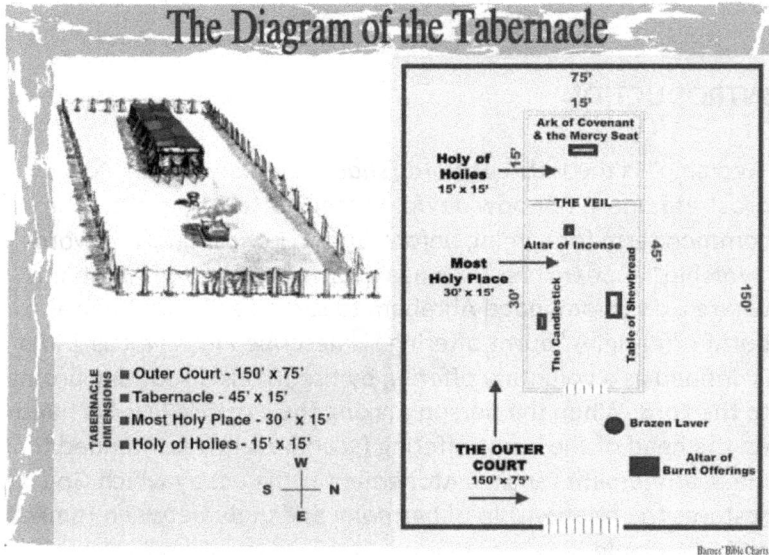

The Diagram of the Tabernacle

Barnes' Bible Charts

The tabernacle was not outwardly attractive! The top cover, made of seal or dolphin skins, was dark and drab. Note that Isaiah 53:2 says . . . *there is no beauty that we should desire Him*. The beauty of Christ was not outward handsomeness, but just as the Tabernacle was drab appearing outside, it was aflame with color on the inside. So it is with Christ. Jesus' attraction was not outward beauty or charisma, but inner purity – a holy inner beauty.

The Tabernacle was a foreshadowing of heavenly things. Moses was admonished by God not to depart in any way from the building instructions he was given. The Israelites camped in the desert around the Tabernacle and night and day they could see the very presence of God when they looked in the direction of the Tabernacle. In addition, everything in the Tabernacle pointed to the coming Messiah, the last sacrificial Lamb.

As one entered the Tabernacle area, the altar and laver were made of brass, which represented judgment. The furniture was made of wood and covered with gold representing Christ's humanity and holiness – it was placed in such a pattern to form a cross. It is described as follows:

Exodus 40:17-33 *In the first month in the second year, on the first day of the month, the tabernacle was erected. 18 Moses erected the tabernacle. He laid its bases, and set up its frames, and put in its poles, and raised up its pillars. 19 And he spread the tent over the tabernacle and put the covering of the tent over it, as the Lord had commanded Moses. 20 He took the testimony and put it into the ark, and put the poles on the ark and set the mercy seat above on the ark. 21 And he brought the ark into the tabernacle and set up the veil of the screen, and screened the ark of the testimony, as the Lord had commanded Moses. 22 He put the table in the tent of meeting, on the north side of the tabernacle, outside the veil, 23 and arranged the bread on it before the Lord, as the Lord had commanded Moses. 24 He put the lampstand in the tent of meeting, opposite the table on the south side of the tabernacle, 25 and set up the lamps before the Lord, as the Lord had commanded Moses. 26 He put the golden altar in the tent of meeting before the veil, 27 and burned fragrant incense on it, as the Lord had commanded Moses. 28 He put in place the screen for the door of the tabernacle. 29 And he set the altar of burnt offering at the entrance of the tabernacle of the tent of meeting, and offered on it the burnt offering and the grain offering, as the Lord had commanded Moses. 30 He set the basin between the tent of meeting and the altar, and put water in it for washing, 31 with which Moses and Aaron and his sons washed their hands and their feet. 32 When they went into the tent of meeting, and when they approached the altar, they washed, as the Lord commanded Moses. 33 And he erected the court around the tabernacle and the altar, and set up the screen of the gate of the court. So Moses finished the work. ESV*

Q1. Based on the above, do you think God cares how we worship Him?

Once the work was done and the Tabernacle was complete, God Himself moved in!

> **Exodus 40:34-37** *Then the cloud covered the tent of meeting, and the glory of the Lord filled the tabernacle. 35 And Moses was not able to enter the tent of meeting because the cloud settled on it, and the glory of the Lord filled the tabernacle. 36 Throughout all their journeys, whenever the cloud was taken up from over the tabernacle, the people of Israel would set out. 37 But if the cloud was not taken up, then they did not set out till the day that it was taken up.* ESV

For 500 years God dwelt among His people in the tabernacle – then He moved! God moved to the temple built by Solomon, but during the final siege of Jerusalem (586 BC) the cloud of God's presence left Solomon's temple, never to return. When the Jews returned from exile in Babylon and rebuilt the temple, God's presence did not return to the Holy of Holies. The glory of His presence was not seen again until:

> *And the Word became flesh and dwelt among us,*
> *and we have seen his glory, glory as of the only Son*
> *from the Father, full of grace and truth.*
> (John 1:14 ESV)

Q2. In the Old Testament the glory of the Lord is linked to the manifest presence of God in the tabernacle. Based on the following passages where or how is God's glory revealed?

John 1:14:

1 Corinthians 6:19-20):

SECTION 2 – The Priest and Atonement

Israel needed a priest who could mediate for them in this place of worship. The priest was to handle the sacrifices in a manner acceptable to God, thus restoring man's relationship with God. In their function of offering sacrifices at the altar, priests acted as mediators between man and God, offering sacrifices so that sin might be forgiven (Leviticus 4:20,26,31). Each sacrifice was a demonstration that the penalty for sin was death (Ezekiel 18:4,20), and that *forgiveness of sin cannot be granted without the shedding of blood* (Hebrews 9:22).

> **Leviticus 9:7** *Then Moses said to Aaron, "Draw near to the altar and offer your sin offering and your burnt offering and make atonement for yourself and for the people, and bring the offering of the people and make atonement for them, as the Lord has commanded." ESV*

Atonement means that we are reconciled to God. The blood of Jesus covers our sin, just as the blood sacrifices in the Old Testament covered the sins of the people making it possible for sinful man to approach a holy God.

> **Hebrews 8:1-2** *. . . we have such a high priest, one who is seated at the right hand of the throne of the Majesty in heaven, 2 a minister in the holy places, in the true tent that the Lord set up, not man.* ESV

Under the new covenant Jesus became our High Priest, serving in the true tabernacle (tent). The tabernacle built by Israel was only a copy patterned after the one in heaven. The office of priest was fulfilled in Jesus Christ. The Son of God became a man (Hebrews 2:9-14) so that He might offer Himself as a sacrifice "once to bear the sins of many" (Hebrews 9:28). Therefore, there is no longer a need for priests to offer a sacrifice to atone for man's sin. A permanent and lasting sacrifice has been made by Jesus Christ through His death on the cross.

Q3. Who are the priests today?

Q4. Knowing that you are a "priest," how should that affect your worship?

SECTION 3 – Enter His Courts With Praise

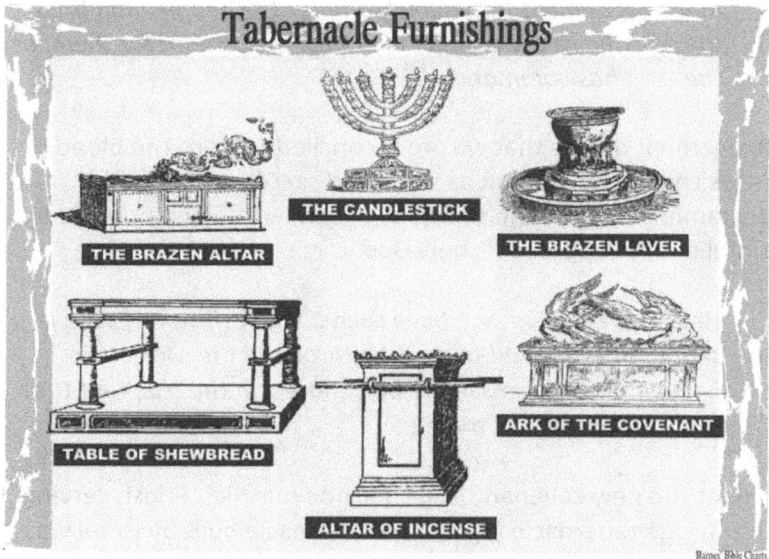

Tabernacle Furnishings

THE CANDLESTICK

THE BRAZEN ALTAR

THE BRAZEN LAVER

TABLE OF SHEWBREAD

ALTAR OF INCENSE

ARK OF THE COVENANT

Barnes Bible Charts

THE GATEWAY

If we review the rules of the tabernacle (Exodus 40:33) we will note that worshippers were to enter through only one place, or the "gateway of the court" (East end). Observe in the following how Jesus fulfills the requirement of how and where to enter into the presence of God.

> **John 10:9, 14:6** *I am the door. If anyone enters by me, he will be saved and will go in and out and find pasture. . . . 14:6 Jesus said to him, "I am the way, and the truth, and the life. No one comes to the Father except through me.* ESV

Q5. How would this apply to worship? Can a person worship God correctly without Jesus?

BRONZE ALTAR

The first thing the worshipper encountered after entering the tabernacle is the bronze altar. The first nine chapters of Leviticus describe seven different offerings to be brought to the bronze altar – we are interested only in the burnt offering in this study.

> **Leviticus 1:3-5** *If his offering is a burnt offering from the herd, he shall offer a male without blemish. He shall bring it to the entrance of the tent of meeting, that he may be accepted before the Lord. 4 He shall lay his hand on the head of the burnt offering, and it shall be accepted for him to make atonement for him. 5 Then he shall kill the bull before the Lord, and Aaron's sons the priests shall bring the blood and throw the blood against the sides of the altar that is at the entrance of the tent of meeting.* ESV

Q6. Who brought the offering? What did he do, and where?

Q7. This is the first piece of furniture or station in the tabernacle. What does that tell us about approaching God to worship Him?

Hebrews 10:4, 10-12 *For it is impossible for the blood of bulls and goats to take away sins. . . . 10 And by that will we have been sanctified through the offering of the body of Jesus Christ once for all. 11 And every priest stands daily at his service, offering repeatedly the same sacrifices, which can never take away sins. 12 But when Christ had offered for all time a single sacrifice for sins, he sat down at the right hand of God.* ESV

Q8. What did Jesus' accomplish and for how long?

BRONZE LAVER (Basin)

Every priest in the tabernacle was required to wash his hands and his feet before beginning his official duties using the bronze laver (Exodus 30:19ff). Note when and why the priest was to wash himself.

Exodus 30:18-20 *You shall also make a basin of bronze, with its stand of bronze, for washing. You shall put it between the tent of meeting and the altar, and you shall put water in it, 19 with which Aaron and his sons shall wash their hands and their feet. 20 When they go into the tent of meeting, or when they come near the altar to minister, to burn a food offering to the Lord, they shall wash with water, so that they may not die.* ESV

Q9. What does this passage from the Psalms tell us about worshipping a holy God?
Psalms 24:3-4 *Who shall ascend the hill of the Lord? And who shall stand in his holy place? 4 He who has clean hands and a pure heart, who does not lift up his soul to what is false and does not swear deceitfully.* ESV

Those who wanted to worship were required to have clean hands and a pure heart! Additionally this psalm warns against sinful behavior and the psalmist mentions both a serious act (idol worship) and a much lessor sin, like swearing falsely. The implication is that all sins, big and small, are considered rebellion against God. But the good news for the new Testament believer is that, *"If we confess our sins, he is faithful and just to forgive us our sins and to cleanse us from all unrighteousness."* (1 John 1:9 ESV)

Q10. Based on 1 John 1:9, what is our responsibility if we sin, and what will God do?

If one is not cleansed properly and worships anyway, it is unacceptable because it is not correct. The result based on Exodus 30:20 is that we die: *When they go into the tent of meeting, or when they come near the altar to minister, to burn a food offering to the Lord, they shall wash with water, so that they may not die.* ESV

Q11. How would you summarize the requirements to come before God in worship?

In Ephesians 5:26, Paul says that Christ gave Himself for the church "that he might sanctify it having cleansed it by the washing (Greek "laver") of water with the word"; and in Titus 3:5 he says that we are saved "through the washing (Greek "laver") of regeneration and renewing of the Holy Spirit." Paul further describes giving our lives as a living sacrifice: *"I appeal to you therefore, brothers, by the mercies of God, to present your bodies as a living sacrifice, holy and acceptable to God, which is your spiritual worship."* (Romans 12:1 ESV) The conclusion of Romans 12:1 follows Paul's full and detailed explanation of the gospel – life, death, resurrection in Romans 1-11. In 12:1 the reference is to a "living" sacrifice.

Q12. Do you believe that true worship can occur without our response to Romans 12:1?

SUMMARY

We have seen how the priest entered the gate, went to the altar (where he assisted in the sacrifices) and washed in the laver (basin). This is a pattern for how a sinful man must approach a holy God. There was only one way to come to God – through the gateway – and *Jesus* is our gate or door. If we are to come before God we must be cleansed from our sin through a sacrifice requiring blood (which has been fulfilled by Christ's death on the cross) and in addition wash ourselves with the Word. We are then regenerated by the Holy Spirit, while offering our whole lives (bodies) as living sacrifices.

SECTION 4
Tent of Meeting – The Holy Place

The tabernacle had two major sections: the outer court and the Tent of Meeting. The Tent of Meeting is technically the inner tent and was further divided into the Holy Place and the Holy of Holies (most holy).

TABLE OF SHOWBREAD

Holy or consecrated bread was placed in the sanctuary of the tabernacle every Sabbath. The showbread symbolized the continual presence of God – a presence more vital than one's daily bread and a dependence on God's provision for their spiritual and physical needs. There were 12 loaves representing the 12 tribes of Israel – all of equal size. The bread was pierced to allow quick and thorough baking, just as Christ, the Living Bread, was pierced on the cross.

The bread in the Tabernacle:

> **Leviticus 24:8-9** *Every Sabbath day Aaron shall arrange it before the Lord regularly; it is from the people of Israel as a covenant forever. 9 And it shall be for Aaron and his sons, and they shall eat it in a holy place, since it is for him a most holy portion out of the Lord's food offerings, a perpetual due.* ESV

> **Exodus 25:30** *And you shall set the bread of the Presence on the table before me regularly.* ESV

The bread of life:

> **John 6:35, 48-51** *Jesus said to them, "I am the bread of life; whoever comes to me shall not hunger, and whoever believes in me shall never thirst. . . . 48 I am the bread of life. 49 Your fathers ate the manna in the wilderness, and they died. 50 This is the bread that comes down from heaven, so that one may eat of it and not die. 51 I am the living bread that came down from heaven. If anyone eats of this bread, he will live forever. And the bread that I will give for the life of the world is my flesh."* ESV

The promise connected to eating this bread is eternal life. The believer will never hunger or thirst. Jesus again speaks of bread in Matthew 4:4 when He says, *"'Man shall not live by bread alone, but by every word that comes from the mouth of God.'"* (ESV) Jesus is comparing the bread to the Scriptures – God's Word.

Q13. What is the lesson or application for us?

Q14. Note who ate the bread of the Presence in the Old Testament. What meaning would that have to us as worshippers in the New Testament (today's priests)?

THE GOLDEN LAMPSTAND

The purpose of the candlestick (lampstand) was to give light in the holy place. It was the only source of artificial light. The lamps were lite in the evening and burned till the morning (Exodus 30:7-8; Leviticus 24:3; 1 Samuel 3:3; 2 Chronicles 13:11). The candlestick here, like the seven candlesticks in Revelation 1:20-21, symbolizes the church of God. In its Old Testament reference, the idea conveyed was that God's church is to be a light giver in the world.

The Lampstand produced light for the Table of Showbread and Altar of Incense. John 8:12 says Jesus is the light to the world and in the four gospels Christ is referred to as the "light" over 20 times. There were no windows to let in light in the Tabernacle, thus the only light came from the Lampstand – there was no need for other light than the light of Christ.

> **Leviticus 24:2-3** *Command the people of Israel to bring you pure oil from beaten olives for the lamp, that a light may be kept burning regularly. 3 Outside the veil of the testimony, in the tent of meeting, Aaron shall arrange it from evening to morning before the Lord regularly. It shall be a statute forever throughout your generations.* ESV

John 8:12 I Am the Light of the World
Again Jesus spoke to them, saying, "I am the light of the world. Whoever follows me will not walk in darkness, but will have the light of life." ESV

Thus, Jesus is the light and gives His followers the light of life!

Q15. What significance is the fact that the lampstand was the only light in the holy place?

ALTAR OF INCENSE

Sweet incense was to be burnt daily at every daily sacrifice, so that a cloud of smoke would fill the inner chamber at the moment when the sacrificial blood was sprinkled. In the book of Revelation, an altar is described as "the golden altar which was before the throne." The incense produced smoke which represented the prayers of the saints that went up before God. This imagery is in harmony with the statement in Luke that as the priests burnt incense "the entire multitude of people were praying." (Luke 1:10).

> **Revelation 8:3-4** *And another angel came and stood at the altar with a golden censer, and he was given much incense to offer with the prayers of all the saints on the golden altar before the throne, 4 and the smoke of the incense, with the prayers of the saints, rose before God from the hand of the angel.* ESV

The incense offered represented an aspect of Christ's suffering, and it was to be offered perpetually (Exodus 30:8), just as Jesus makes perpetual intercession on our behalf.

Leviticus 16:12-13 *And he shall take a censer full of coals of fire from the altar before the Lord, and two handfuls of sweet incense beaten small, and he shall bring it inside the veil 13 and put the incense on the fire before the Lord, that the cloud of the incense may cover the mercy seat that is over the testimony, so that he does not die.* ESV

Q16. How would you describe the purpose of this altar?

Q17. What happens if no incense was taken inside the veil. What does this say about worshiping a Holy God?

SUMMARY

We learn that Jesus is the bread of life and we are to feed on His word. Jesus is described as light and we are to walk as children of light so that He is glorified. Finally, since the incense burns continually we are never to stop praying, which is consistent with Paul's command in 1 Thessalonians 5:17 to pray continually.

SECTION 5
Holy of Holies

The Holy of Holies is the name given to the innermost shrine, or sanctuary. It is the "most holy place" of the tabernacle. It was divided from the holy place by a veil which was lifted when entrance was made. It contained no furniture except the Ark of the Covenant, covered by a slab of gold called the Mercy Seat.

The veil or curtain separated the Tent of Meeting into two areas. It was made of linen and embroidered with angels. Angels were also part of Christ's ministry. There is no evidence that this curtain was 4-6 inches thick as that used in the Temple, which later would be torn in two from top to bottom at the time of Jesus' crucifixion. That tearing signified that we are no longer excluded from the Holy of Holies. Hebrews 10:19-20 says, *"Therefore, brothers, since we have confidence to enter the Most Holy Place by the blood of Jesus, by a new and living way opened for us through the curtain, that is, his body,"* (NIV)

ARK OF THE COVENANT
MERCY SEAT

The Ark of the Covenant represented the presence of God. The Mercy Seat was the place where the Lord "dwelled" and where He communicated with Moses. The Ark contained the stone tables with the Ten Words (commandments) through which God had made known to His people His ethical character.

Once a year the High Priest sprinkled blood from a sacrificial lamb over the Mercy Seat while all of Israel stood outside. Christ is called the "Mercy Seat" in John and in Romans (in both situations the word for "mercy" seat is translated "propitiation"). The blood sprinkled on the Mercy Seat was to atone for (cover) the sins of the people until Christ, the Lamb of God, would shed His blood on the cross to remove our sins once for all time.

And you shall put the mercy seat on the top of the ark,
and in the ark you shall put the
testimony that I shall give you.
Exodus 25:21 ESV

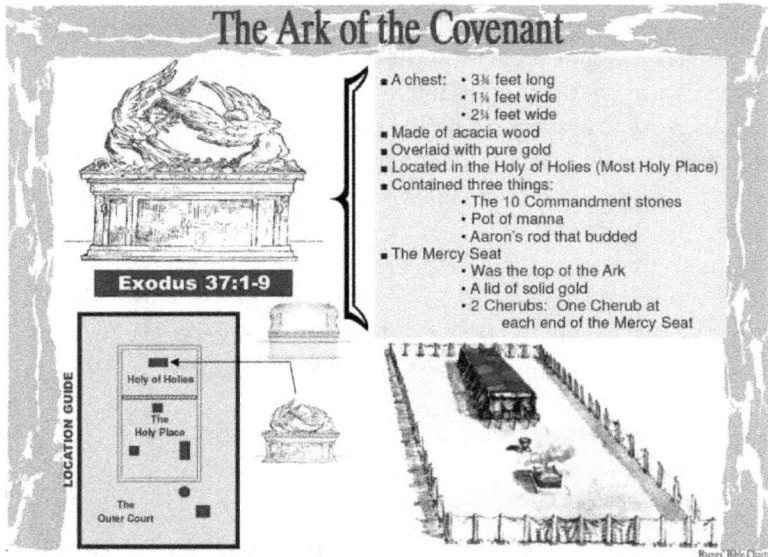

The Ark of the Covenant

- A chest:
  - 3¾ feet long
  - 1¼ feet wide
  - 2¼ feet wide
- Made of acacia wood
- Overlaid with pure gold
- Located in the Holy of Holies (Most Holy Place)
- Contained three things:
  - The 10 Commandment stones
  - Pot of manna
  - Aaron's rod that budded
- The Mercy Seat
  - Was the top of the Ark
  - A lid of solid gold
  - 2 Cherubs: One Cherub at each end of the Mercy Seat

Exodus 37:1-9

MERCY SEAT: The blood of the sacrifice, sprinkled on the Mercy Seat on the great Day of Atonement, allowed reconciliation between God and His people. In Romans 3:25 Jesus is set forth as "a propitiation in His blood," thus fulfilling the idea of the Mercy Seat (compare Hebrews 9:5, 7, 11-12).

The priest entered the Holy of Holies once each year on the Day of Atonement (Yom Kippur). Today, although the Jewish people celebrate Yom Kippur, it is not celebrated in the way prescribed in Leviticus 16 because there is no temple.

Hebrews 9:11-12 Redemption Through the Blood of Christ
But when Christ appeared as a high priest of the good things that have come, then through the greater and more perfect tent (not made with hands, that is, not of this creation) 12 he entered once for all into the holy places, not by means of the blood of goats and calves but by means of his own blood, thus securing an eternal redemption. ESV

Hebrews 9:24-25 *For Christ has entered, not into holy places made with hands, which are copies of the true things, but into heaven itself, now to appear in the presence of God on our behalf. 25 Nor was it to offer himself repeatedly, as* *the high priest enters the holy places every year with blood not his own.* ESV

1 John 2:2 *He is the propitiation for our sins, and not for ours only but also for the sins of the whole world.* ESV

Jesus is the "atoning sacrifice" (propitiation) which indicates the way our sins are covered. Because Jesus paid for our sins in full, God's holiness requirements are satisfied. Thus, Jesus becomes our mercy seat (atonement cover) and the method for paying our sin debt in full, which is sufficient for all time.

Hebrews 10:19-23 The Full Assurance of Faith
Therefore, brothers, since we have confidence to enter the holy places by the blood of Jesus, 20 by the new and living way that he opened for us through the curtain, that is, through his flesh, 21 and since we have a great priest over the house of God, 22 let us draw near with a true heart in full assurance of faith, with our hearts sprinkled clean from an evil conscience and our bodies washed with pure water. 23 Let us hold fast the confession of our hope without wavering, for he who promised is faithful. ESV

The Ark of the Covenant represented the throne or very presence of God. The curtain separated the priest and the people from the presence of God. Only once a year, on the Day of Atonement, could the throne be approached and then only by the priest (never by the people).

At the moment Jesus died on the cross, the veil in the Temple split in half, from top to bottom – a supernatural event. From that moment on there is nothing of any kind separating man from the presence of God. Therefore, we may now openly approach God ourselves. No priest is necessary.

CONCLUSION

Because of the completed work of Christ, our sin is covered once and for all and we can enter into the very throne room of

God. Our grateful response is that that we come worshipping Him, presenting our lives as a living sacrifice which is now holy and acceptable to God!

In summary, our focus should be on what the tabernacle foreshadows: Christ!

Layout:	Shape of cross
Showbread:	Christ as the bread of life
Alter:	Christ's cross
Incense:	Christ as our intercessor
Laver:	Christ's cleansing
Veil:	Christ's human body
Lampstand:	Christ as the light of life
Ark:	Christ's humanity and deity
Mercy seat:	Christ's throne of grace

DISCUSSION QUESTIONS

Given what we learned in Lessons 1 and 2, one might list the requirements for worship today as follows:

a. We must do it right – God has specific requirements.
b. We must enter worship, or approach God through Christ because He is the gate.
c. We must be cleansed, forgiven, purified: free of sin.
d. We must be holy as He is holy.
e. We must bring a sacrifice: our lives.
f. We must be rooted/washed/sustained by the Word.
g. Our heart attitude needs to be right.
h. We need to come in prayer.

1. What do you conclude from the list above?

2. What is the minimum we can bring to worship and be found acceptable?

3. What does God want based on Isaiah 1:16-17?
Isaiah 1:16-17 *Wash and make yourselves clean. Take your evil deeds out of my sight! Stop doing wrong, 17 learn to do right! Seek justice, encourage the oppressed. Defend the cause of the fatherless, plead the case of the widow.* NIV

3A. What did God want? What was the desired behavior?

3B. How is this different than what you listed in #1 above?

3C. Why does Isaiah give this list of "requirements?" See Isaiah 1:12-15.

4. What is the basic underlying condition that motivates your personal worship? Why do you personally come to a worship service on Sunday morning?

5. Could you argue that "obedience is the central issue in worship?" Explain.

6. Given all we have read and discussed it seems evident that we must worship God: (a) with a focus on Christ, (b) with a clean and repentant heart, (c) with a contrite and humble spirit, and (d) with it being holy and rooted in the Word. If you don't believe these are absolute requirements for worship, then what is required or acceptable? Explain.

7. THOUGHT QUESTION: How committed are you, *really*, to worshipping God as He requires?

8. What do you conclude about the subject of worship? Summarize what you have learned from this lesson and list any concerns, questions, or conclusions that have surfaced about present day worship.

WHAT DO I WANT TO REMEMBER?

Enter some notes and information that you want to remember about this lesson. It might be a Scripture verse or two, something new you learned, something you want to do, something you want to change, or just something you want to be sure to remember.

Wisdom to Action
Challenge

In light of Christ's completed work, what aspect of your life can you offer as a "living sacrifice" to God this week? How will this act of worship demonstrate your gratitude?

Lesson 4
the Sabbath

Worship the Lord in the splendor of holiness;
tremble before him, all the earth!
Say among the nations, "The Lord reigns!
Yes, the world is established; it shall never be moved;
he will judge the peoples with equity."
Let the heavens be glad, and let the earth rejoice;
let the sea roar, and all that fills it;
Palm 96:9-11 ESV

SPECIAL NOTE: We will not discuss the specific issue of whether or not the Christian church is _required_ to keep the Sabbath as outlined to Moses. Our focus in this study is to learn about and relate the Old Testament Sabbath requirements to the subject of worship.

KEY SCRIPTURE PASSAGE

Exodus 20:8-10, 31:13-14 *Remember the Sabbath day, to keep it holy. 9 Six days you shall labor, and do all your work, 10 but the seventh day is a Sabbath to the Lord your God. On it you shall not do any work, you, or your son, or your daughter, your male servant, or your female servant, or your livestock, or the sojourner who is within your gates. . . . 13 You are to speak to the people of Israel and say, 'Above all you shall keep my Sabbaths, for this is a sign between me and you throughout your generations, that you may know that I, the Lord, sanctify you. 14 You shall keep the Sabbath, because it is holy for you. Everyone who profanes it shall be put to death. Whoever does any work on it, that soul shall be cut off from among his people. ESV*

HISTORY

A weekly Sabbath is suggested at several places in the Bible, long before the Ten Commandments were given at Mt. Sinai.

The word Sabbath is found in (Exodus 16:21-30), where it describes the giving of manna. While Israel was wandering around in the desert God was planting the idea and concept of a Sabbath rest. He established special requirements for gathering the manna over the Sabbath.

The Sabbath day was part of the foundational Mosaic Law. In fact, each division of the Law contained specific sections relating to the Sabbath. The Law was often described in terms of the moral law (Ten Commandments), the civil law, and the ceremonial law. If one broke the Sabbath Law, there were serious consequences. It was considered sin and outright rebellion. Exodus 21:14 called for the penalty of death for those breaking the Sabbath Law. It was to be a day of rest and all other normal activity was to cease so the follower had nothing to distract his focus from God.

During the period Israel lived under the Law, religious leaders added significantly to the requirements. They wanted to ensure absolute obedience so some of the man-made regulations got a bit frustrating. But they thought they were doing something that would help the people observe the Law. These man-made regulations caused the Law to be a burden rather than an enlightenment.

MEANING OF THE SABBATH

The proper meaning of "Sabbath" is "rest after labor." Sabbath rest is a time for God's people to think about and enjoy what God has accomplished. God's people are instructed to keep the Sabbath because God desired that they rest and use that time to consider their great and awesome God.

The Sabbath rest foreshadows the ultimate salvation that God will provide for His people. He will deliver His people from sin at the end of the age through the Perfect Sacrifice and Redeemer. It includes the idea and practice of celebration. God declared that His Sabbath was a day for public convocation (Leviticus 23:3), a special time to meet together in corporate worship to celebrate their Almighty King (Exodus 31:13).

The concept of celebration also describes the Sabbath as a delight (Psalm 92; Isaiah 58:13; Hosea 2:11). The festivals surrounding the holy days provided rest for everyone (Exodus 23:21; Numbers. 15:32). These holy days also were to be characterized by great rejoicing (food and drink) before the Lord. Thus, God provided that both morning and evening sacrifices were doubled on the weekly Sabbath day (Numbers 28:9; Psalm 92).

On the Sabbath the Showbread, which reminded Israel of God's daily and bounteous blessings was to be replaced. The people were to gather to praise God and to be taught His law (Leviticus 10:11; Deuteronomy 14:29; 33:10).

Q1. What are some examples, other than sports, of how we have compromised Sunday?

Q2. Can you think of some modern day examples of how the church has compromised the Faith?

Q3. Do you think we are compromising the gospel or our faith by the way we treat the Sabbath (Sunday)?

Q4. What is the message of 1 Samuel 2:30?

Therefore the LORD, the God of Israel, declares: 'I promised that your house and your father's house would minister before me forever.' But now the LORD declares: 'Far be it from me! Those who honor me I will honor, but those who despise me will be disdained. NIV

Today the attitude toward Sunday (the Lord's Day) has changed. Sunday is certainly not considered holy by many. The Sunday Blue Laws about working on Sunday have been revoked. Activities on Sunday are no longer thought of in terms of a covenant with God. It's more important to have fun or even work than honor God. When these laws/practices changed, Christians briefly protested, but soon joined the world's values, indicating our conviction was rather superficial. Today for many of families Sunday is a day for organized sports: (1) TV; (2) children leagues; (3) golf; (4) NFL, PGA, NASCAR, etc.

Whether you totally agree with all of the above, it is quite obvious that our attitude as a nation about the focus of Sunday has changed over the past 50-75 years.

Q5. How serious do you view this issue? Why? What do you suggest?

Q6. One of the dangers the Bible describes are rules made by men that prevent the heart from being impacted. Biblically this is worship "in vain." Based on what you know of God's commands concerning the Sabbath, how are you doing?

Q7. Do you think the church is breaking God's rules in any way concerning the Sabbath? Are we not doing something we should? Are we doing something that should be stopped?

DISCUSSION QUESTIONS

1. Scripture says we are a covenant people: chosen, called, and separated (holy) from all other peoples. Do you think of yourself in these terms? Why? Why not?

2. Based on Exodus 31:13-16 what are the ways we demonstrate our covenant with God?
Exodus 31:13-16 *"Say to the Israelites, 'You must observe my Sabbaths. This will be a sign between me and you for the generations to come, so you may know that I am the LORD, who makes you holy. 14 "'Observe the Sabbath, because it is holy to you. Anyone who desecrates it must be put to death; whoever does any work on that day must be cut off from his people. . . . celebrating it for the generations to come as a lasting covenant." NIV*

3. What does it mean that the Sabbath is "*holy*?" What must we do to make Sunday holy?

4. What impact could God have on your life if you set aside the Sabbath (Sunday) as holy (set apart and dedicated to Him)?

ASIDE:

There are at least three things we might focus on in worship:
- To acknowledge the He alone is LORD
- To acknowledge that He is the Creator
- To acknowledge that Jesus is our Redeemer.

How would your worship change if you seriously acknowledged these three beliefs in worship?

5. What could we do to acknowledge Jesus as:

- Lord:

- Creator:

- Redeemer:

6. What does Isaiah say can happen if we honor worship?

Isaiah 58:13-14   *13 "**If** you keep your feet from breaking the Sabbath ·
and from doing as you please on my holy day, if you call the Sabbath a
delight and the LORD's holy day honorable, and if you honor it by not
going your own way and not doing as you please or speaking idle
words, 14 **then** you will find your joy in the LORD, and I will cause you
to ride on the heights of the land and to feast on the inheritance of
your father Jacob." The mouth of the LORD has spoken.* NIV

IF:

THEN:

SUMMARY

We can honor God and keep the Sabbath by:
- Being obedient. (What is the nature of that obedience?)
- Making it a sign to other believers and non-believers so they watch and learn.
- Keeping it holy.
- Resting and not working.
- True worship: delight in Him.

The Sabbath is about God, for God, and because of God.

WHAT DO I WANT TO REMEMBER?

Enter some notes and information that you want to remember about this lesson. It might be a Scripture verse or two, something new you learned, something you want to do, something you want to change, or just something you want to be sure to remember.

Wisdom to Action
Challenge

How can you intentionally create space for rest and reflection on God's goodness in your schedule this week? What specific practice will help you honor the Sabbath principle?

Lesson 5
God Requires a Sacrifice!

*"When we discover the biblical perspective
on worship of God we reach perhaps an
even stronger conclusion: Worship without
sacrifice is really not worship at all."*
David Jeremiah (*My Heart's Desire*)

*I will sacrifice fat animals to you
and an offering of rams;
I will offer bulls and goats.*
Psalms 66:15 NIV

A pig and a chicken were walking together down a country road when they came upon a small country church with a big sign out in the yard: "*HAM AND EGG BREAKFAST – TOMORROW MORNING*" The chicken said to the pig, "I have a great idea, let's both go into the church and make a contribution." But the pig answered, "For you Chicken, it's only a contribution, but for me it's a sacrifice!"

This old story illustrates the seriousness of a sacrifice. A sacrifice is a potentially costly matter. We may make a contribution of money, talent, time, or any number of things without experiencing much real inconvenience. However, we do not make a sacrifice without some pain or cost.

In the Old Testament one of the basic principles of sacrifice was the giving of life (animals) or the products of one's livelihood (grain) to God. God condemned the practice of the pagan cultures that practiced human sacrifice. In its place Israel was instructed to use grain or animals to illustrate the Biblical principle of: substituting one thing for another. The Israelite presented the life of an animal as a substitute and thus fulfilled his sacrificial obligations. The story of Abraham illustrates the principle of substitution in a highly dramatic fashion when God asked Abraham to sacrifice his only son (Genesis 22).

CAIN AND ABLE

In the story of Cain and Abel, we are told that "*In the course of time Cain brought some of the fruits of the soil as an offering to the LORD. 4 But Abel brought fat portions from some of the firstborn of his flock. The LORD looked with favor on Abel and his offering, 5 but on Cain and his offering he did not look with favor. So Cain was very angry, and his face was downcast.*" (Genesis 4:3-5 NIV)

We find that Cain brought a bloodless sacrifice ("he brought fruit of the ground") and Abel brought a bleeding lamb. We must assume that God would have provided a way for men to come to Him, and that way was the way that Abel came. Cain came to God with a sacrifice of his own, choosing, in his own way. So we find men and women in our churches today, coming to God with a sacrifice, not in God's way, but in their own— coming with their own good deeds, or their works, or their own perceived righteousness, and ignore the Lamb altogether. They completely ignore the requirements of the blood because they don't want to come that way. They want to come in their own fashion and on their own terms. Cain may have reasoned that he didn't see why the products of the earth (the fruit) shouldn't be just as acceptable to God as a bleeding lamb. So he brought his fruit.

We don't know how or why there was a difference between these two sons. Both must have been brought up in the same way, both came from the same parents, yet we find in the offering there was a difference between them. One came with the blood, and the other without the blood. Only the one with the blood sacrifice was acceptable to God.

One might wonder why God would receive a "disgusting" sacrifice from Abel and reject a more "respectable" sacrifice from Cain? The answer is most likely because of the horrible nature of sin. The violence of man against God can only be atoned for by the violence of the shedding of blood. The first sacrifice in the world was the one in which God shed the blood of animals in order to provide garments of skin for Adam and Eve to wear after they sinned and they realized they were naked (Genesis 3:21).

The shedding of blood is the pattern God established for covering sin. Abel came to God through the shed blood of his animal sacrifice while Cain brought a respectable offering which he had produced with his own hands that was not acceptable to God.

CHRIST

Hebrews 9:11-14 *When Christ came as high priest . . . 12 He did not enter by means of the blood of goats and calves; but he entered the Most Holy Place once for all by his own blood, having obtained eternal redemption. 13 The blood of goats and bulls and the ashes of a heifer sprinkled on those who are ceremonially unclean sanctify them so that they are outwardly clean. 14 How much more, then, will the blood of Christ, who through the eternal Spirit offered himself unblemished to God, cleanse our consciences from acts that lead to death, so that we may serve the living God!* NIV

SACRIFICE (Exodus 29:1-14)

1. Select the proper animal (Exodus 29:1).

The animals required for any of the sacrifices were to be perfect and without blemish. This symbolized the devotion and commitment of the one making the offering as he presented his gift of life to God. It also reminded the one bringing the sacrifice of his own impurities.

> **Isaiah 53:7-12** *He was oppressed and afflicted, yet he did not open his mouth; he was led like a lamb to the slaughter,*

and as a sheep before her shearers is silent, so he did not open his mouth. 8 By oppression and judgment he was taken away. And who can speak of his descendants? For he was cut off from the land of the living; for the transgression of my people he was stricken. 9 He was assigned a grave with the wicked, and with the rich in his death, though <u>he had done no violence, nor was any deceit in his mouth.</u> 10 Yet it was the LORD's will to crush him and cause him to suffer, and though the LORD makes his life a guilt offering, he will see his offspring and prolong his days, and the will of the LORD will prosper in his hand. 11 After the suffering of his soul, he will see the light [of life] and be satisfied; by his knowledge my <u>righteous servant</u> will justify many, and he will bear their iniquities. 12 Therefore I will give him a portion among the great, and he will divide the spoils with the strong, because he poured out his life unto death, and was numbered with the transgressors. For <u>he bore the sin of many</u>, and made intercession for the transgressors. NIV

Jesus, the perfect sacrifice, fulfilled for all time the expectations of the ancient Israelite believer.

2. Laying on of hands (Exodus 29:10).

The laying on of hands (e.g. Genesis 48:13-16; Exodus 29:10; Deuteronomy 34:9) symbolized the transfer of something from one subject to another. Most instructive in this regard is the example of the "scapegoat" sacrifice on the Day of Atonement (Leviticus 16:21-22). It is obvious here that the laying on of hands is the symbolic transfer of sin from the offeror to the sacrifice.

Isaiah 53:6 *All we like sheep have gone astray; we have turned everyone to his own way; and the Lord has laid on him the iniquity of us all.* ESV

1 Peter 2:24 *He himself bore our sins in his body on the tree, that we might die to sin and live to righteousness. By his wounds you have been healed.* ESV

3. Slaying the animal (Exodus 29:11).

The actual slaying of the animal constituted the most climatic scene of the entire "drama." It symbolized the profound truth that sinners are worthy of death, but it also provided that a divine substitute (ordained by God) would be acceptable in the eyes of God.

> **Isaiah 53:5, 7-8, 12** But _he was pierced for our transgressions, he was crushed for our iniquities;_ the punishment that brought us peace was upon him, and by his wounds we are healed. . . . 7 He was oppressed and afflicted, yet he did not open his mouth; he was _led like a lamb to the slaughter,_ and as a sheep before her shearers is silent, so he did not open his mouth. 8 By oppression and judgment he was taken away. And who can speak of his descendants? For _he was cut off from the land of the living;_ for the transgression of my people he was stricken. . . . 12 Therefore I will give him a portion among the great, and he will divide the spoils with the strong, because he _poured out his life unto death,_ and was numbered with the transgressors. For he bore the sin of many, and made intercession for the transgressors. NIV [All these descriptions applied to Jesus: Romans 4:25; 1 Corinthians 15:3; Hebrews 9:28]

As the slaughter was central in the Old Testament sacrifice, so was the crucifixion of Jesus in the New. Paul summarizes this fact when he concludes his sermon at Corinth: _For I decided to know nothing among you except Jesus Christ and him crucified._ (1 Corinthians 2:2 ESV)

4. The priestly use of blood (Exodus 29:12).

The importance assigned to the blood and the elaborate procedures surrounding its use are both distinctive and instructional. The pouring of the blood on the altar symbolized the forgiveness of sin (Leviticus 17:11 – life is in the blood). The application of blood coincides with the cancellation of sin. In Biblical terms this may be referred to as _"expiation"_ or the act of obliterating the stain of sin and removing it from the sight of God.

> **Isaiah 53:5** *But he was pierced for our transgressions, he was crushed for our iniquities; the punishment that brought us peace was upon him, and <u>by his wounds we are healed</u>.* NIV

> **1 John 1:7** *But if we walk in the light, as he is in the light, we have fellowship with one another, and the <u>blood of Jesus, his Son, purifies us from all sin.</u>* NIV

The significance of the sacrificial blood for the Christian is sharply outlined in Romans 3:23-25.

> **Romans 3:23-25** *for all have sinned and fall short of the glory of God, and are justified freely by his grace through the redemption that came by Christ Jesus. God presented him as a <u>sacrifice of atonement</u>, through faith in his blood. He did this to demonstrate his justice, because in his forbearance he had left the sins committed beforehand unpunished.* NIV

5. Consecration (Exodus 29:13).

In the Old Testament process the additional burning of the entrails of the animal was intended not to destroy but to produce a more refined act that would delight the heart of God. For example:

> **Exodus 29:18** *Then burn the entire ram on the altar. It is a burnt offering to the LORD, <u>a pleasing aroma</u>, an offering made to the LORD by fire.* NIV

This process was concluded when the worshipper symbolized his willingness to consecrate himself to God by offering to Him specified portions of the animal he had brought to the sacrifice.

For the New Testament Christian, the voluntary sacrifice of Christ was one glorious act of consecration. Paul may have said it best in Ephesians 5:2 . . . *Christ loved us and gave himself up for us as a fragrant offering and sacrifice to God.* NIV

OUR SPIRITUAL ACT OF WORSHIP

Romans 12:1-2 *Therefore, I urge you, brothers, in view of God's mercy, to offer your bodies as living sacrifices, holy and pleasing to God-this is your spiritual act of worship. Do not conform any longer to the pattern of this world, but be transformed by the renewing of your mind. Then you will be able to test and approve what God's will is – his good, pleasing and perfect will.* NIV

Notice if you break this passage down into the key phrases:

- offer your body (life) as a living sacrifice
- it should be holy and pleasing to God
- it is a spiritual act of worship
- do not be conformed to the values of the world
- we are to be transformed by the renewing of our mind
- THEN . . .

Paul is speaking about everyday life. Most people today are being conformed to this world. The world is squeezing us into the shape and character it desires. But God's desire is that reshaping does not happen. God wants us to be an offering to Him. It's no easy matter to live His way. We're required to be obedient. We're required to submit to God and to sacrifice each moment, each relationship, each trial, and each setting to Him. It's a great deal easier to go to church and simply submit an offering envelope. But God wants a greater sacrifice than that. He wants it all.

Your marriage needs to be offered up as a sacrifice every single day. So does your parenting. So does the way you spend your free time. Your job, your relationships, your recreation, your rest – all should be an offering to God. If you began to make a list of the things you could offer up in sacrifice, you might never stop writing. The truth is that when your life becomes a temple, a home for Jesus, you begin to see His face in the faces of all those who surround you. You begin to treat them as you would treat Him. You begin to realize that all ground is holy ground, because God is there. You begin to see every situation as a potential act of worship, a time or opportunity to magnify the name of the Lord.

We who live in a comfortable generation want good things to come without paying the price. We want the result without the work. We want the feast without the sacrifice. We want resurrection Sunday without the pain of Good Friday. But the Scriptures tell us things never work out that way. Whenever we want something worthwhile and eternal, we must always pay a price. Unless we're willing to pay the price, we can't experience those eternal things.

Everything worthwhile is built on some kind of sacrifice. Creating strong homes and churches takes sacrifice as believers stand up for moral purity in a world polluted with immorality. Supporting the work of ministry requires sacrifice as Christians forego some worldly pleasures in order to fund the work of God in the world. Nothing good ever comes easily, and if we do not have those willing to sacrifice, the ministry of the church will disappear in the world.

The apostle Paul calls this a living sacrifice, "holy, acceptable to God" (Romans 12:1). He's talking about much more than giving up television or chocolate milkshakes for Lent. Presenting ourselves as a holy sacrifice means surrendering ourselves on the altar of God. We hold nothing back. We attach no strings. And yet every ounce of our sinful nature tells us to be selfish and be the captain of our own soul. It hurts to lay ourselves down on that altar.

DISCUSSION QUESTIONS: Romans 12:1-2

Romans 12:1-2 A Living Sacrifice
I appeal to you therefore, brothers, by the mercies of God, to present your bodies as a living sacrifice, holy and acceptable to God, which is your spiritual worship. 2 Do not be conformed to this world, but be transformed by the renewal of your mind, that

by testing you may discern what is the will of God, what is good and acceptable and perfect. ESV

1. What are the implications about the will of God?

2. In what ways do we tend to conform to the world?

3. How will the renewing of our minds happen?

4. What five things (characteristics) in Romans 12:1-2 does Paul say are needed for our personal sacrificial offering?

5. Do these five things describe how you feel about worship?

DISCUSSION QUESTIONS: General

1. In Genesis 4:6-7 where it says that "sin is crouching at the door" what makes our offerings and worship acceptable or unacceptable to God?

2. Why did God require a blood sacrifice?

> We should recognize that God is requiring a live sacrifice in the Old Testament. These are not dead animals being brought to the altar. Thus, He wants a *living sacrifice* from us.

1 Peter 1:23-2:5

Since you have been born again, not of perishable seed but of imperishable, through the living and abiding word of God; 24 for "All flesh is like grass and all its glory like the flower of grass. The grass withers, and the flower falls, 25 but the word of the Lord remains forever." And this word is the good news that was preached to you.

A Living Stone and a Holy People
2:1 So put away all malice and all deceit and hypocrisy and envy and all slander. 2 Like newborn infants, long for the pure spiritual milk, that by it you may grow up to salvation 3 if indeed you have tasted that the Lord is good. 4 As you come to him, a living stone rejected by men but in the sight of God chosen and precious, 5 you yourselves like living stones are being built up as a spiritual house, to be a holy

priesthood, to offer spiritual sacrifices acceptable to God through Jesus Christ. ESV

Note in 1 Peter 1:23 above the basis or foundation of our salvation is "the abiding word of God."

3. Why is the word "abiding" important here?

4. What are the steps outlined (in 2:1) in order that we can offer "spiritual sacrifices acceptable to God identified in (2:5)"?

5. Based on the following verses, what are the spiritual offerings (sacrifices) being suggested?

Philippians 2:17 *Even if I am to be poured out as a drink offering upon the sacrificial offering of your faith, I am glad and rejoice with you all.* ESV _____

Philippians 4:18 *I have received full payment, and more. I am well supplied, having received from Epaphroditus the gifts you sent, a fragrant offering, a sacrifice acceptable and pleasing to God.* ESV _____

Romans 12:1 *I appeal to you therefore, brothers, by the mercies of God, to present your bodies as a living sacrifice, holy and acceptable to God, which is your spiritual worship.* ESV _____

Hebrews 13:15 *Through him then let us continually offer up a sacrifice of praise to God, that is, the fruit of lips that acknowledge his name.* ESV _____

Romans 15:16 *to be a minister of Christ Jesus to the Gentiles in the priestly service of the gospel of God, so that* *the offering of the Gentiles may be acceptable, sanctified by the Holy Spirit.* ESV _____

6. What is God looking for in those who worship Him?

7. Based on 1 Peter 2:1 how is this worship to be accomplished?

These questions raise the obvious concern: What spiritual preparation are we making before we come to a Worship Service?
Do you think God accepts your worship?

---

8. Read Psalm 15. How do we meet these requirements?
Psalm 15 *O Lord, who shall sojourn in your tent? Who shall dwell on your holy hill? 2 He who walks blamelessly and does what is right and speaks truth in his heart; 3 who does not slander with his tongue and does no evil to his neighbor, nor takes up a reproach against his friend; 4 in whose eyes a vile person is despised, but who honors those who fear the Lord; who swears to his own hurt and does not change; 5 who does not put out his money at interest and does not take a bribe against the innocent. He who does these things shall never be moved.* ESV

CONCLUSION: From these Scriptures we can draw the conclusion that our modern day worship must be focused on Christ and His Word. I think it is safe to say that social issues, life issues, political issues, economic issues, etc. should not be the focus of our preaching *unless* the issues can be related to Christ and His teachings which are directed toward the church, not the community or the government. In order to be a living sacrifice we must be prepared, Christ-centered, and able to function as a "living stone."

9. What are the implications of Isaiah 1:13-15?
Isaiah 1:13-15 *Bring no more vain offerings; incense is an abomination to me. New moon and Sabbath and the calling of convocations—I cannot endure iniquity and solemn assembly. 14 Your new moons and your appointed feasts my soul hates; they have become a burden to me; I am weary of bearing them. 15 When you spread out your hands, I will hide my eyes from you; even though you make many prayers, I will not listen; your hands are full of blood.* ESV

Q. Do you think there is anything in the New Testament that would make us exempt from bringing worship that is acceptable?

10. Based on this week's lesson, make a list of the things that you believe God accepts and those things He rejects:

Worship God Accepts   Worship God Rejects

11. Why do you come to church on Sunday morning? What are you expecting? What do you want?

WHAT DO I WANT TO REMEMBER?

Enter some notes and information that you want to remember about this lesson. It might be a Scripture verse or two, something new you learned, something you want to do, something you want to change, or just something you want to be sure to remember.

Wisdom to Action
Challenge

Identify an area of your life you've been holding back from God. What step can you take to surrender this area as a "living sacrifice" in worship?

Lesson 6
God is Central!

THE TEN COMMANDMENTS

Exodus 20:3-11 *You shall have no other gods before me. 4 You shall not make for yourself a carved image, or any likeness of anything that is in heaven above, or that is in the earth beneath, or that is in the water under the earth. 5 You shall not bow down to them or serve them, for I the Lord your God am a jealous God, visiting the iniquity of the fathers on the children to the third and the fourth generation of those who hate me, 6 but showing steadfast love to thousands of those who love me and keep my commandments. 7 You shall not take the name of the Lord your God in vain, for the Lord will not hold him guiltless who takes his name in vain. 8 Remember the Sabbath day, to keep it holy. 9 Six days you shall labor, and do all your work, 10 but the seventh day is a Sabbath to the Lord your God. On it you shall not do any work, you, or your son, or your daughter, your male servant, or your female servant, or your livestock, or the sojourner who is within your gates. 11 For in six days the Lord made heaven and earth, the sea, and all that is in them, and rested the seventh day. Therefore the Lord blessed the Sabbath day and made it holy.* ESV

Note that the first four commandments above are all about God and worship. God speaks to Moses and to Israel for the first time in 400 years and the first four things are about Himself and the nature of worship:

- no other gods,
- no idols,
- not take God's name in vain, and
- honor the Sabbath.

THE FOCUS IS GOD – He must be central

Mark 12:28-30 . . . *"Of all the commandments, which is the most important?" 29 "The most important one," answered Jesus, "is this: 'Hear, O Israel, the Lord our God, the Lord is one. 30 Love the Lord your God with all your heart and with all your soul and with all your mind and with all your strength.'"* NIV

God's plan is that all have a chance to be saved. His desire is that all would come to know the saving power of Christ. If His people love Him with all their heart, that will manifest itself into loving one another and taking the Gospel to the world. He wants the whole world to know. Thus, Jesus is to be the central focus of our lives:

> **John 1:4, 9** *In him was life, and that life was the light of men . . . 9 The true light that gives light to every man was coming into the world.* NIV

> **John 6:63** *The Spirit gives life; the flesh counts for nothing. The words I have spoken to you are spirit and they are life.* NIV

Q1. What are we doing if we allow "other gods" in our life?

We must personally be very cautious if we worship at the altar of other gods! What we are doing indicates we have no respect for God! What songs are we singing? What words are we speaking? Worshipping other gods would certainly mean worship of the Lord was in vain.

Q2. If a stranger watched you for a month, who or what would they say you worshipped? How have you spent your time and your money? Where have you invested your talents? What are your priorities?

There is a quick check you can do to answer this question. Pull out your datebook and answer the following questions:

1) How much time did you spend on
religious activities last month? _____ hrs.
2) How much time did you spend
reading the Bible? _____ hrs.
3) How much time did you spend
watching TV or recreational reading? _____ hrs.
4) How much time did you spend
participating in a hobby, recreation, or leisure? _____ hrs.
5) How much time did you spend on
your phone, the internet, or social media? _____ hrs.

Did you bring your first fruits to God? Yes? No?

Q3. What can you conclude about your priorities concerning your faith? Is God central in your life, or not?

Q4a. If your answers above are not what you want them to be, what must you do to improve the result? What would it take to change your behavior?

It's probably accurate to conclude that the quality of your worship will be in direct proportion to how well you know God. Therefore, how much time are you spending with God in prayer or reading His Word?

Jeremiah 9:23-24 *Thus says the Lord: "Let not the wise man boast in his wisdom, let not the mighty man boast in his might, let not the rich man boast in his riches, 24 but let him who boasts boast in this, that he understands and knows me, that I am the Lord who practices steadfast love, justice, and righteousness in the earth. For in these things I delight, declares the Lord."* ESV

Q4b. What can <u>you</u> boast about?

Q5. What do the following say it means to know Christ?

1 John 5:20 *And we know that the Son of God has come and has given us understanding, so that we may know him who is true; and we are in him who is true, in his Son Jesus Christ. He is the true God and eternal life.* ESV

1 John 2:3 *And by this we know that we have come to know him, if we keep his commandments.* ESV

1 John 2:6 *whoever says he abides in him ought to walk in the same way in which he walked.* ESV

1 John 4:21 *And this commandment we have from him: whoever loves God must also love his brother.* ESV

Q6. Do you know Christ based on the verses above?

List the characteristics or activities in your life that demonstrate you know Him.

NOTE:

If you must argue your case about knowing Him, what is your evidence? Jesus reported that there would be people doing "miracles" that didn't know Him:

Matt 7:22-23 *Many will say to me on that day, 'Lord, Lord, did we not prophesy in your name, and in your name drive out demons and perform many miracles?' 23 Then I will tell them plainly, 'I never knew you. Away from me, you evildoers!'* NIV

CONSIDER:

How much time do you spend thinking about religious things, about your walk with Christ, about your service or ministry, your calling, your gifts, your witness, the church, your eternal significance, the lost . . . . Remember, God's primary concern is not your job, your family, your home, your health, or even your service . . . it's the condition of your heart toward Him! Do you know Him as your Lord and Savior?

TEST:

Do you obey, walk as He did, love your brother? If so, somebody should have noticed? Who noticed?

Q7. Based on the following three passages, why should you want to know Christ?

a. _____

2 Thessalonians 1:8 *in flaming fire, inflicting vengeance on those who do not know God and on those who do not obey the gospel of our Lord Jesus.* ESV

b. _____

Galatians 4:8-10 *Formerly, when you did not know God, you were enslaved to those that by nature are not gods. 9 But now that you have come to know God, or rather to be known by God, how can you turn back again to the weak and worthless elementary principles of the world, whose slaves you want to be once more? 10 You observe days and months and seasons and years!* ESV

c. _____

Philippians 3:10-11 *that I may know him and the power of his resurrection, and may share his sufferings, becoming like him in his death, 11 that by any means possible I may attain the resurrection from the dead.* ESV

Consider the Parable of the Ten Virgins (Matthew 25:1-13). Do you remember their problem? They were not prepared and they were not known when they returned with the oil they needed. The result was that they were excluded from His presence.

"How do you want Jesus to find you on His return?"

We often think we are above the fray because we are one of the people teaching Sunday school, ushering, acting as the liturgist, singing in the choir . . . I don't want to get you upset, but this is serious business. The people in Mt 7:23-23 were doing serious ministry (miracles), and they didn't really know Christ! Do you know Him, or do you just know about Him?

Exercise

List up to ten things that prove or demonstrate that you know Christ and He knows you:

1

2

3

4

5

6

7

8

9

10

BE HOLY BECAUSE HE IS HOLY

> *But just as he who called you is holy,*
> *so be holy in all you do; for it is written:*
> *"Be holy, because I am holy."*
> 1 Peter 1:15-16 NIV

In worship we are (or should be) reminded of His holiness, which means our own sin is often obvious or revealed to us. When we recognize the holiness of our God, we can often seem pretty inadequate:

> **Psalms 99:9** *Exalt the Lord our God, and worship at his holy mountain; for the Lord our God is holy! ESV*

> **Revelation 4:8** *And the four living creatures, each of them with six wings, are full of eyes all around and within, and day and night they never cease to say, "Holy, holy, holy, is the Lord God Almighty, who was and is and is to come!" ESV*

Q8. Does God's holiness impact the worship in your life or in your church?

If, YES – How?

If, NO – Why not?

In worship God may draw us to Himself, revealing our sin. Do you believe that happens in worship? Is that your experience? Are you ever convicted of your sinful nature during a Worship Service?

Q9. What are your typical barriers to worship? What would it take to remove them?

<u>Barriers</u>   <u>How Remove</u>

- sin   ____confession and repentance ____
- misuse of God's name   _____
- other priorities – God not #1 _____
- broken relationships(Mt 5:23-24)_____
- idols (other gods)   _____
- no thoughts about God   _____
- keeping the Sabbath   _____
- _____   _____
- _____   _____
- _____   _____

Q10. How does <u>your</u> worship demonstrate or show that:

- God is holy:

- God hates sin:

- God redeems:

- God grants life:

- God requires obedience:

- God blesses obedience:

- God grants great mercy and grace:

- God grants His people power and boldness:

Are you satisfied with your answers above?
Do you ever see worshippers trembling before a Holy God? Is anyone worried about their sin or their unworthiness? Does the entire congregation ever sense the awesome sovereign nature of God? Does anyone fear a righteous holy God?

Q11. Do you ever feel the greatness of God in worship?

ASIDE:
What does "hallowed be your name" mean to you and what does it indicate in the Lord's Prayer? You might answer that His Name is above every name because:

- We are called by His name (2 Chronicles 7:14)
- We gather in His name (Matthew 18:20)
- We pray in His name (John 14:13-14)
- We live by faith in His name (Acts 3;16)
- We proclaim His name (Exodus 9:16)
- We are baptized in his name (Matthew 28:19)
- We put hope in His name (Matthew 12:21)

Q12. How would you suspect God reacts to disinterested worship given the following two verses?
Acts 4:12 *Salvation is found in no one else, for there is no other name under heaven given to men by which we must be saved.* NIV
Colossians 3:17 *And whatever you do, whether in word or deed, do it all in the name of the Lord Jesus, giving thanks to God the Father through Him.* NIV

PSALM 145

If you want to better understand the greatness of God, read Psalm 145 and absorb what it says about the nature of God and what it says we are to do:

Verse	What we learn about God
3:	God is great; worthy of praise
5:	God is majestic; He does wonderful works
6:	God demonstrates power in His works; His deeds are great
7:	God's goodness is abundant; God is righteous
8:	He is gracious, compassionate; slow to anger
9:	He is good to all; compassion
11/12:	His Kingdom is glorious; He is mighty
13:	His Kingdom is everlasting; it will endure forever; He is faithful and loving
14:	He upholds and lifts up all who are down
15:	He provides food
16:	He satisfies desires of all living things
17:	He is righteous; loving
18:	He will be near to those who call on Him in truth
19:	He fulfills desires of those who fear Him; He saves those who fear Him
20:	He watches over those who love Him; destroy wicked
21:	He is holy

Q13. What are we to do in response to the above in Psalm 145?

Verse	What do
1:	
2:	

4:

5:

6:

7:

10:

11:

18:

19:

20:

21:

WHAT DO I WANT TO REMEMBER?

Enter some notes and information that you want to remember about this lesson. It might be a Scripture verse or two, something new you learned, something you want to do, something you want to change, or just something you want to be sure to remember.

Wisdom to Action
Challenge

Examine your priorities. What competing focus in your life needs to be realigned to ensure God remains central? How will you practically make this shift this week?

EXHIBIT – God's Attributes

Have you ever been at a loss for what to pray or how to praise God? You can never go wrong praising God for His character and nature:

1. God the Creator. Creator God, I praise You because you made the heavens, even the highest heavens, and all their starry host, the earth and all that is on it, the seas and all that is in them. You give life to everything and the multitudes of heaven worship you. (Neh 9:6)

2. Only God. God, I praise You because You are the LORD, and there is no other. Apart from You there is no God. (Isa 5:5)

3. An Almighty God. O LORD God Almighty, who is like you? You are mighty, O LORD, and your faithfulness surrounds you. (Ps 89:8)

4. An Everlasting Father. I praise You, Lord, as the Ancient of Days and the Everlasting Father, who lives forever and ever.

 5. A Loving God. I praise You because You are a loving God, whose very nature is love. (I Jn 4:16).

6. A God of justice. Lord, I magnify You, because you are just and the one who justifies those who have faith in Jesus. (Ro 3:26)

7. A Faithful God. Heavenly Father, I give You my praise and adoration, because You are a faithful God, keeping Your covenant of love to a thousand generations of those who love You and keep Your commands. (Dt 7:9)

8. A Merciful God. You are a gracious and merciful God and I praise You for Your great mercy.

9. God, My Refuge, My Fortress. I praise You, Lord, for You are my mighty rock and my refuge. (Ps 62:7)

10. A Patient, Persevering God. Father, I praise You because You are patient with Your children, not wanting anyone to perish, but everyone to come to repentance. (2 Pet 3:9). Thank You for Your patience with me.

11. Eternal, Saving God. I give praise to You, Father, 'he only God our Savior. To You be glory, majesty, power and authority, through Jesus Christ our Lord, before all ages, now and forevermore. (Jude 25)

12. The Holy One. Holy, holy, holy are You Lord God Almighty, who was, and is, and is to come. (Rev 4:8)

13. Personal God. I praise You, because You are a personal God, who gives me the honor of knowing You, even inviting me to feast at Your kingdom's table with Abraham, Isaac, and Jacob. (Mt 8:11)

14. Giving God. All praise and honor be Yours, O God. You are a generous God, who did not stop short in giving us Your Son. (Jn 3:16)

15. A Provider God. I praise You today, Lord, as my Jehovah-Jireh (provider), who makes all grace abound in me and generously provides all I need. (2 Cor 9:8)

16. God, My Shepherd. I bless Your name and praise You as my Jehovah-Rohi (shepherd), who will shepherd me and guide me in the paths of righteousness for Your name's sake. (Ps 23:1-3)

17. God, My Victory. Praise to You, my God, because You are my Jehovah-Nissi (my banner), who always leads me in triumphal procession in Christ. (2 Cor 2:14)

18. God, My Peace. I praise You with all my heart, Lord, because You are my Jehovah-Shalom (our peace), the God of peace who will soon crush Satan under His feet. (Ro 16:20)

19. The God Who Heals. Father, I praise You because You are the Lord who heals me. (Ex 15:26)

20. The God of All Comfort. Praise be to the God and Father of our Lord Jesus Christ, the Father of compassion and the God of all comfort. (2 Cor 1:3)

21. God of Miracles. Lord, I praise You because You perform miracles; you display your power among the peoples. (Ps 77:14)

22. Forgiving God. I want to bless You with praise, Father, because you are a forgiving God, gracious and compassionate, slow to anger, and abounding in steadfast love. (Neh 9:17)

23. The Burden Bearer. Praise be to the Lord, to God my Savior, who daily bears my burdens. (Ps 68:19)

24. A Faithful God. I praise You because your love, O LORD, reaches to the heavens, your faithfulness to the skies (Ps 36:5). Great is your faithfulness. (Lam 3:23)

25. King of Kings. All honor and praise be to You, my God, the blessed and only Ruler, the King of kings and Lord of lords, who alone is immortal and who lives in unapproachable light. (1 Tim 6:15)

26. God the Liberator. I will praise You because you are my help and my deliverer. (Ps 70:5)

27. The Lifter of My Head. Father God, I praise You because you are a shield around me; you bestow glory on me and lift up my head when I am weary or despised. (Ps 3:3)

28. God of Light. I praise You, Lord, because You are my light and my salvation (Ps 27: 1). You know what lies in darkness, and light dwells with You. (Dan 2:22)

29. God of joy. I give You praise because you have granted me eternal blessings and made me glad with the joy of your presence. (Ps 21:6)

30. The God of All. I praise and adore You. You are the Holy One of Israel, my Redeemer, and the God of all the earth. (Isa 54:5)

Lesson 7
Worship in Spirit and Truth

*"The great sin of the world is that we have failed
to delight in God so to reflect His glory,
because God is most reflected in us
when we are most delighted in Him."*
John Piper

John Piper in his book, *The Supremacy of God in Worship*, says worship, not missions, is the ultimate goal of the church, not missions. Mission work is necessary because worship of God is lacking. God is ultimate, not man. When this age is over and millions fall on their face before God, missions will no longer be necessary. But worship will go on forever. Our aim in missions is to bring the nations into the white-hot enjoyment of God's glory.

**Our goal is the gladness of the
peoples in the greatness of God**!

Passion for God in worship precedes the offer of God in preaching. You can't commend what you don't cherish. One cannot call out, "Let the nations be glad!" who cannot say from the heart, *"I rejoice in the Lord . . . I will be glad and exult in thee, I will sing praise to thy name, O Most High"* (Psalm 104:34; 9:2).

If the pursuit of God's glory is not ordered above the pursuit of man's good, man will not be well served and God will not be duly honored. We should not diminish missions, but we <u>must</u> magnify God. When the flame of worship burns with the heat of God's true worth, the light of missions will reach to all parts of the earth. But where passion for God is weak, zeal for missions will be weak. Churches that are not centered on the exultation of the majesty and beauty of God will hardly kindle a fervent desire to *"declare his glory among the nations"* (Psalm 96:3). Outsiders will see the disparity between the boldness of our claims and the blandness of our engagement with our God.

God must be the central focus of the church. Where people are not stunned by the greatness of God, how can they be sent with the ringing message, *"Great is the Lord and greatly to be praised; he is to be feared above all gods!"* (Psalm 96:4) Savoring the vision of a triumphant God in worship precedes spreading it to others. All of history is moving toward one great goal: the worship of God among the peoples of the earth.

When the glory of God saturates our preaching, teaching, conversation, writing, and when He predominates above our talk of plans and strategies, then the people will begin to feel that He is the central reality of their lives, and that the spread of His glory is more important than personal plans and possessions.[2]

KEY SCRIPTURES

John 4:23-24 *Yet a time is coming and has now come when the true worshipers will worship the Father in spirit and truth, for they are the kind of worshipers the Father seeks. 24 God is spirit, and his worshipers must worship in spirit and in truth."* NIV

- Worship with my whole heart
  Romans 1:9 *God, whom I serve with my whole heart in preaching the gospel of his Son, is my witness how constantly I remember you.* NIV

- Focus on God
  Psalms 86:11 *Teach me your way, O LORD, and I will walk in your truth; give me an undivided heart, that I may fear your name.* NIV
  John 14:6 *Jesus answered, "I am the way and the truth and the life. No one comes to the Father except through me."* NIV

- Worship must be based on God's Word/Truth
  Psalms 119:11 *I have hidden your word in my heart that I might not sin against you.* NIV
  Psalms 119:18 *Open my eyes that I may see wonderful things in your law.* NIV
  Psalms 119:33 *Teach me, O LORD, to follow your decrees; then I will keep them to the end.* NIV

Q1. The passage from John 4:23 says a "time is coming." What "time" is coming?

WHAT IS WORSHIP TO YOU?

What do you immediately think of when someone says "worship"? Most people immediately think of singing on Sunday morning. If you were an avid golfer who "worshipped" the game of golf, what would you be doing? How would you act? What would you say? Where would you go? Let's make a list:

1. I would take lessons and read books on how to improve my game.
2. I would play with great integrity and call penalties on myself.
3. I would truthfully report my scores in the clubhouse.
4. I would play in public view allowing others to see my skill.
5. I would promote the game to others, particularly young people.
6. I would work out to get in the best shape as possible to play well.
7. I would play as much as possible – every chance I could get.
8. I would spend time at the clubhouse when not playing.
9. I would use the BEST equipment and keep it in good shape.
10. I would hire the best caddy to give me advice and carry my clubs.
11. I would watch PGA and LPGA Tours on TV.
12. I would go to Tour events, observe the pros, and cheer them on.

Let's make a list comparable to the above that would represent similar activities for worshipping God:

1. I would be discipled by a mature Christian and I would read the Bible and other Christian literature.

2. I would examine my heart for sin and if found confess it to God.
3. I would be truthful about my struggles and my successes.
4. I would be open about my faith so that others could see my walk with the Lord and be encouraged.
5. I would share my story and testimony with others.
6. I would exercise my mind (Romans 12:1-2) and "rest" on Sunday.
7. I would be in church every Sunday and participate fully in church.
8. I would be at church for special events and learning experiences.
9. I would have a study Bible filled with my hand-written notes.
10. I would have an accountability partner and friend to do life with.
11. I would use TV and the internet to observe authentic spirit-filled worship and preaching.
12. I would visit other churches and go to Christian conferences.

As you think of this comparison, which set of individuals do you associate with having the most passion for their interest? It is certainly interesting how the activities of a golfer line up against those of a Christ-follower and the success in each activity will be greatly determined by the passion one brings to the game!

Worship is an encounter with the living God! If this is true, what do you think it means to "encounter" God? The most probable understanding would be to experience God in some way. You would meet or engage with God, hear from Him, or feel His presence. It might occur while engaged in active ministry for God or participating in local service projects. The encounter is such that one feels very close to God and you may even feel that God is communicating with you in some way.

DELIGHT IN THE LORD

Q2. Based on the following passages, what are we to do and what is the result?

Zephaniah 3:14 *Sing . . . Be glad and rejoice with all your heart, O Daughter of Jerusalem!* NIV

Psalms 37:4 *Delight yourself in the Lord and he will give you the desires of your heart.* NIV

Psalms 73:25 *Whom have I in heaven but you? And earth has nothing I desire besides you.* NIV

Zephaniah 3:14

Psalm 37:4

Psalm 73:25

Delight would mean we have great satisfaction in knowing Him and seeking His presence in our lives. Delight would also include proclaiming His Name to others. If we delight in something we generally want to tell someone about the object of our delight. Delight falls more on the side of joy in the Lord than on happiness in our life walk. We may be experiencing some very difficult times and still delight in the Lord while not being happy enduring life's trials.

As a child we may associate delight with happiness, but as an adult we recognize that is a very flawed understanding.

Q3. If you were to experience true delight how would you describe it?

HIS PRESENCE – Drawing Near

Hebrews 10:19-22 *Therefore, brothers, since we have confidence to enter the holy places by the blood of Jesus, 20 by the new and living way that he opened for us through the curtain, that is, through his flesh, 21 and since we have a great priest over the house of God, 22 let us draw near with a true heart in full assurance of faith, with our hearts sprinkled clean from an evil conscience and our bodies washed with pure water.* ESV (See also Hebrews 12:18-24)

James 4:8 *Draw near to God, and he will draw near to you. Cleanse your hands, you sinners, and purify your hearts, you double-minded.* ESV (See also 2 Chronicles 5:13-14)

Notice that the author of Hebrews calls us to draw near to God and James says that if we draw near to Him He will draw near to us. Does this mean that there is a physical nearness? There could be but the drawing near more likely means there is a personal relationship that is real. We are growing in an intimate relationship and our hearts and minds are focused on being in His will – we are abiding in Christ. This will result in a desire to be obedient to the ways of God that flows out of our intimate relationship. This is described in Psalm 16:11:

> *You make known to me the path of life;*
> *in your presence there is fullness of joy;*
> *at your right hand are pleasures forevermore.* ESV

Based on the passages above, one might conclude that worship is a two-way experience of us seeking the presence of God and God in turn approaching us. I don't think we can say that God is meeting us half-way but there is certainly an indication that God will respond if we make an attempt to seek or approach Him.

There is a great satisfaction in delighting in God that is described by David:

> **Psalm 27:4** *One thing have I asked of the Lord, that will I seek after: that I may dwell in the house of the Lord all the days of my life, to gaze upon the beauty of the Lord and to inquire in his temple.* ESV

TRUE WORSHIP

True worship might be described by the following statements:

1. To lift up and praise the name of Jesus!
2. To exalt and proclaim the supremacy of God.
3. To rejoice and be glad in God; to delight in his presence.
4. To glorify God in mind, body, and spirit.
5. To uphold and display the greatness of God.
6. To pursue the glory of God above all else.
7. To recognize the beauty and majesty of His name.
8. To proclaim the centrality of God in our lives.

9. To praise Him for His acts of power and mighty deeds.
10. To exhibit an excitement for the glory of the King.

In writing and listing these descriptions of worship I have a deep sadness at the state of my own worship. This is an area of my life I need to work on! If you feel the same after reviewing this list, don't despair. God knows we are not perfect yet, but the time will come when every knee will bow and every tongue confess that Jesus is Lord!

WORSHIP IN SPIRIT

Q4. How is worship described in the following?
John 4:23-24 *Yet a time is coming and has now come when the true worshipers will worship the Father in spirit and truth, for they are the kind of worshipers the Father seeks. 24 God is spirit, and his worshipers must worship in spirit and in truth." NIV*

The first question that comes to my mind is, "Why does Jesus make this statement about worshippers?" Remember the context of this statement. The Jews of Samaria and Judah worshipped God on a different basis: (1) they worshipped in different places, Mt Zion versus Mt. Gerizim, (2) the Samaritans believed only in the first five books of the Bible, rejecting the Psalms and Prophets, (3) Israel was the chosen nation (Romans 9:4-5), and (4) In John 3:22 Jesus said the Samaritans worshipped what they did not know.

In John 4 Jesus was announcing that the external form of worship (the location, the physical ceremonial rules of worship) were no longer a priority, but that the internal things (the heart) were God's primary interest. God wanted worship that came come from within our innermost being and not be accomplished by robotically following a set of rules. Jesus was also saying that worship in the temple was no longer a requirement – the rituals, rules, and location were no longer the real issue. Rather, a spiritual connection directly to God through Jesus was now possible.

The methods and focus of worship were changing and what the Law had originally envisioned was going to come to pass:

> **Deuteronomy 30:6** *The Lord your God will circumcise your hearts and the hearts of your descendants, so that you may love him with all your heart and with all your soul, and live.* NIV

Our hearts are to be circumcised and we are to love God with all our heart . . . the Great Commandment of the New Testament. Remember, circumcision was God's declared way or sign of a person aligning himself with the Faith. It symbolized total commitment to the Lord.

The importance of the <u>heart </u>is evident in many passages in the Bible. Note the following:

1. Fear the Lord and serve Him with all your heart.
1 Sam 12:24 *But be sure to fear the LORD and serve him faithfully with all your heart; consider what great things he has done for you.* NIV

The fear of the LORD dreads God's displeasure, desires His favor, reveres His holiness, submits cheerfully to His will, is grateful for His benefits, sincerely worships Him, and conscientiously obeys His commandments. Old Testament fear (loving reverence) has its foundation in love and causes one to endeavor in all things to please God rather than to offend Him. It gives God the place of glory, honor, reverence, thanksgiving, praise, and preeminence he deserves.

2. Praise the Lord from our inmost being (heart).
Psalms 103:1 *Praise the LORD, O my soul; all my <u>inmost being,</u> praise his holy name.* NIV

3. Rejoice in the Lord because your heart is wise.
Proverbs 23:15-16 *My son, if your heart is wise, then my heart will be glad; 16 my inmost being will rejoice when your lips speak what is right.* NIV

4. Be righteous in the Lord and take refuge in Him.
Psalms 64:10 *Let the righteous rejoice in the Lord and take refuge in him; let all the upright in heart praise him!* NIV

Further, Scripture tells us there are four more fundamental things that will be true if we worship God "in Spirit."

1. We will be born of the Spirit – born again (saved).
John 3:6-7 *. . . but the Spirit gives birth to spirit. 7 You should not be surprised at my saying, 'You must be born again.'* NIV

2. We will yield our hearts to His control.
Romans 2:29 *No, a man is a Jew if he is one inwardly; and circumcision is circumcision of the heart, by the Spirit, not by the written code. Such a man's praise is not from men, but from God.* NIV

3. We will respond with repentant and contrite hearts.
Isaiah 66:2 *Has not my hand made all these things, and so they came into being?" declares the LORD. "This is the one I esteem: he who is humble and contrite in spirit, and trembles at my word.* NIV

CONTRITE: The person with a contrite spirit weeps over wrongdoing and expresses genuine sorrow for his sin (see Matthew 5:4; Luke 6:21; 2 Corinthians 7:10). The heart is the seat of our true self, our true feelings of joy or sadness. Therefore, a contrite heart is one in which the natural pride and self-sufficiency of man has been completely humbled by the consciousness of guilt.

4. We have an undivided heart – our focus is on only God.
Psalms 86:11 *Teach me your way, O LORD, and I will walk in your truth; give me an undivided heart, that I may fear your name.* NIV

We should remember that God is spirit, meaning He is invisible, divine, and life-giving. Man's spirit is what will last and it is the spirit that attains intimacy with God. True worship is when man's spirit meets with God's Spirit. God is not physical – He is invisible. This is one of the basic truths of Christianity. Almost all peoples, nations, and religions have had some idea of "God" as material, but the Bible declares that God is spirit.

Thus, our real worship should be internal, not external. It should be spiritual versus consisting of rituals and ceremony like under the Old Covenant. True worshippers will worship the Father in spirit. The worship of the Samaritans was a defective worship – they did not receive the prophetical writings or revelations. Theirs was as an external worship, dealing only in the letter of the law, and at a distance, by rituals and ceremonies.

The preaching of the Gospel communicated the true nature of God and a new salvation. Because of this, it was in opposition to the defective Samaritan worship.

Today, worship is not a matter of ritual, ceremony, liturgy, schedule, or rules (or observation of the Law). Christian worship is a matter of the heart (spirit). It is not the following of outward forms, procedures, or observances, but the true devotion of the spirit – the sincerity of the heart.

Q5. Do you think your church has tried to substitute rites and ceremonies for true worship?

Q6. Since worship is not confined to places, where can it take place?

WORSHIP IN TRUTH

Worship in truth requires that we recognize the foundation of the moral law: The Ten Commandments (Exodus 20:2-9). Acceptable worship means we are engaged in the process and aware that our worship can be unacceptable to a holy God (Hebrews 12:28-29). We must be careful not to worship in vain, that is, with hearts that are not engaged:

Matthew 15:7-9 *You hypocrites! Well did Isaiah prophesy of you, when he said: 8 "This people honors me with their lips, but their heart is far from me; 9 in vain do they worship me, teaching as doctrines the commandments of men."* ESV

John 1:14 *The Word became flesh and made his dwelling among us. We have seen his glory, the glory of the One and Only, who came from the Father, full of grace and truth.* NIV

John 14:6 *Jesus answered, "I am the way and the truth and the life. No one comes to the Father except through me."* NIV

What is the truth that must be worshipped? Wrong question! Who is the truth that must be worshipped? The truth is fundamentally a person – the Lord Jesus Christ. Jesus is the truth and the life. Jesus must be the focus of our worship because He is the truth and the key to our access to God. We access the truth through the power of the indwelling Holy Spirit:

> **John 16:13** *But when he, the Spirit of truth, comes, he will guide you into all truth. He will not speak on his own; he will speak only what he hears, and he will tell you what is yet to come.* NIV

God's Word is also described as truth in both the Old and New Testaments:

> **Psalms 119:160** *All your words are true; all your righteous laws are eternal.* NIV
> **John 17:17** *Sanctify them by the truth; your word is truth.* NIV

Thus, worship under the New Covenant is through Christ, in Christ, and for Christ. No one can worship God except through Christ. That worship is enabled through the Holy Spirit.

> **Romans 11:36** *For from him and through him and to him are all things. To him be the glory forever! Amen.* NIV

To worship in truth is to understand that Jesus is truth and we must worship God through Christ ("in truth"). We cannot be blind to the truth or put our hope in the claims of men. Thus, true worship:

(1) is God-centered,
(2) conforms to the Word, and
(3) puts its hope in the promises of Christ.

Our truth is in Christ, and it recognizes Jesus as Lord and the Messiah. It is the only way to the Father (John 14:6; Acts 4:12).

Q7. What are some of the things that can take your focus off God in our worship?

ACCEPTABLE WORSHIP

We discussed this in depth in Lesson 2, but let's review the basics:

> **Hebrews 12:28** *Therefore, since we are receiving a kingdom that cannot be shaken, let us be thankful, and so worship God acceptably with reverence and awe,* NIV

Remember, your worship must be acceptable to God. Worship is to be done in reverence and awe. When was the last time you stood in your church during worship and were in awe or overwhelmed by the supremacy or greatness of God? Many in the church have lost the awe that should accompany our worship.

What is unacceptable and what happens if our worship is not acceptable? Simply, it is of no real value. It is worthless. UGH! So, what makes worship acceptable? We would summarize the answer to that question as follows:

WHO:	Jesus
WHAT:	the Bible (God's Word)
WHERE:	anywhere
WHEN:	anytime
WHY:	to glorify, exalt, and revere God

This will happen only when our heart is connected to the one true God.

All worship by nature is God-centered because only God-centered worship will bring us face to face with our Holy God! Consequently, it can be fatal for us if our worship becomes man-centered or self-centered.

WORSHIP AS A LIVING SACRIFICE

Again, we have discussed this previously, but we should end this lesson with a reminder that we are a living sacrifice!

God is the object of our worship but with the coming of Christ the nature of a believer's worship changed. Worship is no longer associated with a list of rules, requirements, and ceremonies designed to create devotion. The Lord desires that we worship in spirit and truth.

Our lives are the sacrifice of our true worship. Our lives should be transformed and be pleasing to God. When my worship is a _living_ sacrifice, then I am walking worthy with my God.

The result of a transformed life is the worship of our Savior as Lord and results in a sacrifice of praise:

> **1 Peter 2:5, 9** *You also, like living stones, are being built into a spiritual house to be a holy priesthood, offering spiritual sacrifices acceptable to God through Jesus Christ . . . 9 But you are a chosen people, a royal priesthood, a holy nation, a people belonging to God, that you may declare the praises of him who called you out of darkness into his wonderful light.* NIV

CONCLUSION

We are to be overwhelmed by the greatness of God, have a white-hot passion for God, be excited about God, or have our soul occupied with God. What does all that mean? I describe it as follows:

- He saturates my being.
- He is constantly before me.
- He is foremost in my thoughts.
- He is the first thing I think about in the morning and the last thing at night.

What would cause us to have something described as a white-hot passion for God? That passion must start with a deep internal understanding in our hearts and minds that He did for us what we could not do for ourselves. He Himself paid the penalty for our guilt. He even paid the penalty before He made His righteousness available to us. Thus, in our hearts we can fully know and understand who He is, and what He has done. We should rejoice in that knowledge.

The psalmist may describe the nature of our worship best:

> **Psalms 96:9-13** *Worship the LORD in the splendor of his holiness; tremble before him, all the earth. 10 Say among the nations, "The LORD reigns." The world is firmly established, it cannot be moved; he will judge the peoples with equity. 11 Let the heavens rejoice, let the earth be glad; let the sea resound, and all that is in it; 12 let the fields be jubilant, and everything in them. Then all the trees of the forest will sing for joy; 13 they will sing before the LORD, for he comes, he comes to judge the earth. He will judge the world in righteousness and the peoples in his truth.* NIV

We are commanded to worship because He is holy and worthy of our worship. When He judges the world in righteousness and truth it will have to include the nature of our worship.

In summary we must remember the five important requirements for worshipping in "spirit and truth."

1. It must be God-centered.
2. It is enabled by the Holy Spirit.
3. It is in conformity to God's Word (made flesh in Christ).
4. It requires a relationship with Jesus, who is the truth.
5. It requires my heart to be committed.

But if we do not follow the instructions and desires of God, it can be in vain and unacceptable.

DISCUSSION QUESTIONS

1. Do you worship with your whole heart? Do you ever hold back in any way?

2. What are the major distractions <u>you</u> experience when trying to worship?

3. What is the meaning and implication of Ephesians 5:26, "*that he might sanctify her, having cleansed her by the washing of water with the word,*" ESV

4. What do you do regularly to prepare for Sunday Worship?

5. Given Philippians 3:3, how would you describe worship?
Philippians 3:3 *For we are the real circumcision, who worship by the Spirit of God and glory in Christ Jesus and put no confidence in the flesh.* ESV

6. Given Mark 7:7-8, which says, "*in vain do they worship me, teaching as doctrines the commandments of men. 8 You leave the commandment of God and hold to the tradition of men.*" ESV Have you ever evaluated the way you worship? For example, what about:

- your preparation?
- what you sing (the words)?
- what you pray?
- how you dress?
- your demeanor in church?
- your body language?
- your priorities?

WHAT DO I WANT TO REMEMBER?

Enter some notes and information that you want to remember about this lesson. It might be a Scripture verse or two, something new you learned, something you want to do, something you want to change, or just something you want to be sure to remember.

Wisdom to Action
Challenge

Do you prepare to meet the Most Holy God
when you worship?

Lesson 8
Worship in Heaven

REVELATION 4:1-11

1 After this I looked, and there before me was a door standing open in heaven. And the voice I had first heard speaking to me like a trumpet said, "Come up here, and I will show you what must take place after this."
2 At once I was in the Spirit, and there before me was a throne in heaven with someone sitting on it.
3 And the one who sat there had the appearance of jasper and carnelian. A rainbow, resembling an emerald, encircled the throne.
4 Surrounding the throne were twenty-four other thrones, and seated on them were twenty-four elders. They were dressed in white and had crowns of gold on their heads.
5 From the throne came flashes of lightning, rumblings and peals of thunder. Before the throne, seven lamps were blazing. These are the seven spirits of God.
6 Also before the throne there was what looked like a sea of glass, clear as crystal. In the center, around the throne, were four living creatures, and they were covered with eyes, in front and in back.
7 The first living creature was like a lion, the second was like an ox, the third had a face like a man, the fourth was like a flying eagle.
8 Each of the four living creatures had six wings and was covered with eyes all around, even under his wings. Day and night they never stop saying:

> *"Holy, holy, holy*
> *is the Lord God Almighty,*
> *who was, and is, and is to come."*

9 Whenever the living creatures give glory, honor and thanks to him who sits on the throne and who lives for ever and ever, 10 the twenty-four elders fall down before him who sits on the throne, and worship him who lives for ever and ever. They lay their crowns before the throne and say: 11 "You are worthy, our Lord and God, to receive glory and honor and power, for you created all things, and by your will they were created and have their being." NIV

Revelation was written when Christians were in a time of persecution and needed encouragement. It was most likely written either during Nero's time (AD 54-68) or during Domitian's reign (AD 81-96). Most scholars date the writing around 95 AD, about 60 years after the resurrection of Christ.

In Chapters 2-3 of Revelation, Christ described the church ("universal") to John in the form of seven letters to various individual churches in Asia Minor. Christians who proclaimed Jesus as Lord (not Caesar) were facing increased hostility. The Roman authorities wanted to enforce worship of the emperor. John wrote to encourage the faithful to resist the demands of emperor worship. The church was under great pressure and persecution to bow to Caesar.

What did the lethargic, spoiled, sinful churches described in Revelation 2-3 need? They needed a vision, and Jesus, through the Apostle John, provided that encouragement. John told of the heavens being opened up in Chapters 4-5 so the church could compare the way things were to the way they will be. John was given a vision of God sitting on His throne. The message to the reader is that the throne was <u>not</u> empty.

Based on what John saw and what we can conclude from his writing, can learn a lot about authentic worship. There seems to be no question or hesitation in the hearts of the 24 elders as to how they should respond at the awesome sight of God. Not only is there praise but there is submission. It is one thing to <u>intellectually</u> recognize the authority of God, but it is another to <u>actively respond</u>, demonstrating one's true commitment and allegiance.

DOORS

Revelation 3:8 *I know your deeds. See, I have placed before you an <u>open door</u> that no one can shut. I know that you have little strength, yet you have kept my word and have not denied my name.* NIV

Revelation 3:20 *Here I am! I stand at the <u>door</u> and knock. If anyone hears my voice and opens the door, I will come in and eat with him, and he with me.* NIV

The same Lord who opened the door for believers in the Philadelphia church (3:8) now opens a door for John into the throne room of heaven. God knows that our confidence can be more firmly established with an accurate view of Himself. Jesus speaks with a trumpet-like voice (1:10) and with authority declaring that John is being shown what "must take place."

Revelation 4:1 *After this I looked, and there before me was a door standing open in heaven. And the voice I had first heard speaking to me like a trumpet said, "Come up here, and I will show you what must take place after this."* NIV

VOICE LIKE A TRUMPET

Revelation 1:10 *On the Lord's Day I was in the Spirit, and I heard behind me a loud voice like a trumpet.* NIV

The reference to a trumpet may remind us of what is said about the trumpet call in 1 Corinthians 15:52: *in a flash, in the twinkling of an eye, at the last trumpet. For the trumpet will sound, the dead will be raised imperishable, and we will be changed.* NIV

Many are patiently waiting to hear that trumpet!

THE THRONE

Revelation 4:2 *At once I was in the Spirit, and there before me was a throne in heaven with someone sitting on it.* NIV

John is transported in some manner, described as being "in the Spirit," so that he can see what Jesus wants to show him. The first thing John records is that the throne is occupied (Isaiah 6:1; Psalm 47:8). It is not empty — someone is in charge! The "throne" is mentioned more than forty times in Revelation. God is on the throne and the courts of heaven are in session. It is remarkable at this point that John gives no description of Him who sits on the throne, nor does he indicate who He is by name.

In this context "being in the Spirit" likely means John is caught up in ecstasy, a dream, seeing a vision, or having some real out-of-body experience. It's not the same meaning that Paul is referring to when he says, "in the Spirit." Frankly it's not particularly important to know the exact nature of John's condition, but rather what he saw and experienced.

GOD ON HIS THRONE

Revelation 4:3 *And the one who sat there had the appearance of jasper and carnelian* [sardis]. *A rainbow, resembling an emerald, encircled the throne.* NIV

John is making an attempt here to describe God and he uses precious stones to give us some idea of the brilliance, majesty, and glory that he sees. A rainbow that we see only as an arc encircles the throne, reminding the reader of God's faithfulness and His covenant with Noah. It also may indicate that in heaven all things are complete.

Note that there is no mention of the shape or form of the One sitting on the throne. The description is only in terms of precious stones — maybe what is in view is the brilliance and flashing light produced by those stones. Some have suggested that the stones represent:

- jasper (white) – purity (holiness) of God
- sardian (red) – wrath of God
- emerld (green) – mercy of God

The rainbow around the throne may be intended to signal God's grace.

God on His throne would certainly be an encouragement to John's readers. The precious stones would have been well understood in Jesus' day as representing the stones that were on the breastplate of the High Priest. On the breastplate of the high priest the first and last stones were sardius and jasper (Exodus 28:17, 20). They are mentioned again in the foundation of the New Jerusalem (Revelation 21:19-20).

TWENTY-FOUR ELDERS

Revelation 4:4 *Surrounding the throne were twenty-four other thrones, and seated on them were twenty-four elders. They were dressed in white and had crowns of gold on their heads.* NIV

Next we are told of 24 thrones and 24 elders – who probably represent the church or the totality of the redeemed. Many scholars think that the 24 symbolize the 12 tribes and the 12 apostles of Jesus, but Dr. David Jeremiah believes the 24 represents the body of Christ, just as the 24 priests who ministered daily in the temple (1 Chronicles 24), represented the people. This view is strengthened when you note that:

- The *white garments* are consistent with righteousness and holiness which will be worn by the church (Rev 3:4, 18; 7:9, 19:7-8, 14).
  Revelation 3:4 *Yet you have a few people in Sardis who have not soiled their clothes. They will walk with me, dressed in white, for they are worthy.* NIV
  Revelation 3:18 *I counsel you to buy from me gold refined in the fire, so you can become rich; and white clothes to wear, so you can cover your shameful nakedness; and salve to put on your eyes, so you can see.* NIV

- The *golden crowns* are representative of a royal calling and the reign of Christ (3:21; 4:4; 22:5). They may signal the victory He has won for us.

   Revelation 2:10 *Do not be afraid of what you are about to suffer. I tell you, the devil will put some of you in prison to test you, and you will suffer persecution for ten days. Be faithful, even to the point of death, and I will give you the crown of life.* NIV

   Revelation 3:21 *To him who overcomes, I will give the right to sit with me on my throne, just as I overcame and sat down with my Father on his throne.* NIV

- They are *praising God* (Rev 5:8-9)

   Revelation 5:8-9 *And when he had taken it, the four living creatures and the twenty-four elders fell down before the Lamb. Each one had a harp and they were holding golden bowls full of incense, which are the prayers of the saints. 9 And they sang a new song: "You are worthy to take the scroll and to open its seals, because you were slain, and with your blood you purchased men for God from every tribe and language and people and nation."* NIV

Elsewhere in Revelation we find that the 24 elders are continually worshipping and praising God (5:11, 14; 7:11; 11:16; 14:3; 19:4).

   Revelation 5:14 *The four living creatures said, "Amen," and the elders* *fell down and worshiped.* NIV

   Revelation 7:11 *All the angels were standing around the throne and around the elders and the four living creatures. They* *fell down on their faces before the throne and* *worshiped* *God.* NIV

   Revelation 11:16 *And the twenty-four elders, who were seated on their thrones before God,* *fell on their faces and worshiped God.* NIV

   Revelation 19:4 *The twenty-four elders and the four living creatures fell down and worshiped God, who was seated on the throne. And they cried: "Amen, Hallelujah!"* NIV

CROWNS

A number of crowns are described in Scripture:

The Crown that lasts forever
1 Corinthians 9:25-26 *Everyone who competes in the games goes into strict training. They do it to get a crown that will not last; but we do it to get a <u>crown that will last forever</u>. 26 Therefore I do not run like a man running aimlessly . . .* NIV
(Note that it is the one who participates/competes that gets crown)

Crown of life
James 1:12 *Blessed is the man who perseveres under trial, because when he has stood the test, he will receive the <u>crown of life</u> that God has promised to those who love him.* NIV

Crown of glory
1 Peter 5:2-4 *Be shepherds of God's flock that is under your care, serving as overseers-not because you must, but because you are willing, as God wants you to be; not greedy for money, but eager to serve; 3 not lording it over those entrusted to you, but being examples to the flock. 4 And when the Chief Shepherd appears, you will receive the <u>crown of glory</u> that will never fade away.* NIV

Crown of righteousness
2 Timothy 4:8 *Now there is in store for me the <u>crown of righteousness</u>, which the Lord, the righteous Judge, will award to me on that day – and not only to me, but also to all who have longed for his appearing.* NIV

THUNDER | SEVEN LAMPS | SEA OF GLASS

Revelation 4:5-6a *From the throne came flashes of lightning, rumblings and peals of thunder. Before the throne, seven lamps were blazing. These are the seven spirits of God. 6 Also before the throne there was what looked like a sea of glass, clear as crystal. . .* NIV

This imagery helps us picture the awesome power of God. The thunder and lightning reminds readers of Mt. Sinai (Exodus 19:16-24) and other times that God spoke to His people in a thundering voice. The Spirit of God is again associated with fire as it was at Pentecost. The glass that is clear as crystal may indicate the immensity and serenity of heaven.

John also saw seven lamps of fire, which he identified as symbols of the seven Spirits of God. The seven Spirits of God seems likely to refer to the perfection and fullness of the activities of the Third Person of the Godhead – the Holy Spirit.

There are other times when lightning and thunder are described: Exodus 1:13; Psalm 77:18; Job 37:4; Exodus 19:16. This imagery is all associated with the presence of God.

FOUR LIVING CREATURES

Revelation 4:6b-8 . . . *In the center, around the throne, were four living creatures, and they were covered with eyes, in front and in back. 7 The first living creature was like a lion, the second was like an ox, the third had a face like a man, the fourth was like a flying eagle. 8 Each of the four living creatures had six wings and was covered with eyes all around, even under his wings. Day and night they never stop saying: "Holy, holy, holy is the Lord God Almighty, who was, and is, and is to come."* NIV

Most believe that these four creatures represent the created beings on earth:

- the LION is the king of beasts
- the OX is the king of domesticated animals
- the EAGLE is the king of birds
- the MAN is king of human creation

The four forms suggest what is noblest, strongest, swiftest, and wisest in creation. Nature, including man, is represented before the throne taking its part in the fulfillment of God's divine will – the worship of Himself. We may only guess at some of the meaning of Revelation but it seems very clear here that all creation praises its Creator.

The four creatures are seen elsewhere engaged in praise and worship (Revelation 5:8, 14; 7:11; 19:4) and we see the same faces described in Ezekiel's vision (Ezekiel 1:6,10, 22, 26). The creatures seem to be angelic beings that are always close to God and possibly even guard His throne.

> **Revelation 5:8** *And when he had taken it, the four living creatures and the twenty-four elders fell down before the Lamb. Each one had a harp and they were holding golden bowls full of incense, which are the prayers of the saints.* NIV

Probably the most likely interpretation (again from Dr. David Jeremiah) is that they represent angelic beings who function to bring glory to God. This would be consistent with their description in Ezekiel 1:4-14; 10:14-17; and Isaiah 6:1-3. They are clearly involved with God in two ways:

- They testify to the holiness of God in worship, and
- They execute His judgments on the world as seen in the breaking of the first four seals (Revelation 6:1, 3,5,7; 15:7).

This doxology of praise highlights three aspects of God:

- He is HOLY – different, unique, and set apart. We stand in admiration and awe.

- He is ALMIGHTY (omnipotent) – power beyond all imagination.

- He is ETERNAL (everlasting) – God is forever but man is temporary, like the grass of the field.

The implication is that the ceaseless activity of nature and man under the hand of God is a ceaseless tribute of praise (Psalm 19:1-2; 103:22; 148). One might conclude that if you are fulfilling the function for which you were created, you will praise God. Everyone and everything, nature and man, praise God. The Westminster catechism says that, "Man's chief end is to glorify God and enjoy Him forever." Thus, during work, rest, worship, and even in the most humbling of activities, we should praise God

In Revelation 5:13 every creature praises God. Everyone! All the creatures that have breath praise the Lord.

> **Revelation 5:13** *And I heard <u>every creature</u> in heaven and on earth and under the earth and in the sea, and all that is in them, saying, "To him who sits on the throne and to the Lamb be blessing and honor and glory and might forever and ever!"* ESV

HEAVENLY WORSHIP

Revelation 4:9-11 *Whenever the living creatures give glory, honor and thanks to him who sits on the throne and who lives for ever and ever, 10 the twenty-four elders fall down before him who sits on the throne, and worship him who lives for ever and ever. They lay their crowns before the throne and say: 11 "You are worthy, our Lord and God, to receive glory and honor and power, for you created all things, and by your will they were created and have their being."* NIV

We can conclude from this picture and description that worship is a primary activity of heaven. Not only is worship important but it is an activity that is going on continuously. The phrase "holy, holy, holy" (4:8) is the only description of God that is repeated three times indicating its importance. It most likely refers to God's purity and absolute sovereignty. All of heaven is worshipping God as Creator and Sustainer. The church, represented by the elders, has recognized her Lord and Master.

Note the significant difference in the way that the 4 creatures and the 24 elders worship. The creatures only celebrate and declare, but the elders also fall down before the throne and cast their crowns before God, indicating that they worship with understanding and spiritual intelligence. They know and have experienced the joy of salvation! The elders' worship is that of the redeemed, who knowing and understanding their own unworthiness, intelligently make a decision to enter into the holiness and love of God. They (we) are persons who have been won by His love and grace, we have had our sinful hearts covered by His blood, and we have been accepted because of His promise of grace!

All creation acknowledges the supremacy of God. We learn from this song that He made all things for His pleasure. It seems evident, that He sustains and maintains all that He has made and He certainly has not made man or any created creature to be miserable.

We are given four reasons for our adoration in 4:8-11:

(1) *He is worthy.*

(2) *He is the Creator of all things*: the Creator of all things should be adored and no created thing should be the object of religious worship.

(3) *He is the preserver of all things*, and His preservation is a continual process. All beings but God are dependent upon the will and power of God, and no dependent being should be set up as an object of religious worship.

(4) *He is the final cause of all things*: it was His will and pleasure to create all things.

SUMMARY

In Revelation 4:1-11 Jesus ushers John into the throne room of God and allows John to see what is going on in eternity. John discovers and sees first-hand another reality. This world (Earth) is simply not all there is to reality! Television, radio, magazines, the internet, and newspapers describe one reality: the world. The world is the only reality we see. Our minds are constantly being bombarded by the events of this world.

Yet there is an unseen reality in heaven. Jesus is telling John that all is not centered in this world. John sees the eternal reality that is the eternal praise of the living God. Jesus takes John into the "control room" of heaven and allows him a glimpse of the ultimate reality. John sees that everything is not out of control, Satan has not won, and evil has not triumphed over good. God is on His throne and all is well – the Lamb of God has won!

Lightning plays around the one seated on the throne, flashing on four angelic beings who praise Him day and night, saying: *"Holy, holy, holy is the Lord God Almighty, who was, and is, and is to come."* Just beyond this inner circle are 24 elders, who also worship. They joyfully lay their crowns before the throne and say: *"You are worthy, our Lord and God, to receive glory and honor and power, for You created all things, and by Your will they were created and have their being."*

This is a magnificent scene and one that should bring peace and assurance to John and his readers.

DISCUSSION QUESTIONS

1. If the "elders" represent the church, then what conclusions might you draw about worship in Heaven?

2. What reason is given for this worship? (4:11)

3. What is the significance of laying their crowns before the throne?

4. What does submission mean? Before you answer, review the following:

> **Revelation 4:10** *the twenty-four elders <u>fall down before him</u> who sits on the throne,*
> **Revelation 5:8**. . .*the four living creatures and the twenty-four elders <u>fell down before the Lamb</u>.*
> **Revelation 5:14** *the four living creatures said, "Amen," and the elders <u>fell down</u> and worshiped.*
> **Revelation 7:11-12** *All the angels were standing around the throne and around the elders and the four living creatures. They <u>fell down on their faces</u> before the throne and worshiped God.*
> **Revelation 11:16** *and the twenty-four elders, who were seated on their **thrones before God, <u>fell on their faces</u> and worshiped God.***
> **Revelation 19:4** *the twenty-four elders and the four living creatures <u>fell down and worshiped</u> God, who was seated on the throne.*

5. Why do you suppose John was shown this picture of the elders and not regular disciples?

6. How can we surrender our authority (like the 24 elders) in our worship and in our lives?

7. What does Revelation 22:3 say the saints will be doing in eternity?

Revelation 22:3 *No longer will there be anything accursed, but the throne of God and of the Lamb will be in it, and his servants will worship him. ESV*

Revelation 22:3 *And there shall be no more curse, but the throne of God and of the Lamb shall be in it, and His servants shall serve Him. NKJV*

ESV: _____

NKJV: _____

8. Based on all this, how should we prepare for eternity?

9. Read Psalm 96:7-12 below. Based on this passage, how are we to "ascribe" to the Lord the glory due His name?

Psalm 96:7-12 *Ascribe to the Lord, O families of the peoples, ascribe to the Lord glory and strength! 8 Ascribe to the Lord the glory due his name; bring an offering, and come into his courts! 9 Worship the Lord in the splendor of holiness; tremble before him, all the earth! 10 Say among the nations, "The Lord reigns! Yes, the world is established; it shall never be moved; he will judge the peoples with equity." 11 Let the heavens be glad, and let the earth rejoice; let the sea roar, and all that fills it; 12 let the field exult, and everything in it! Then shall all the trees of the forest sing for joy. ESV*

10. Consider the following questions.
There is a saying that goes, "You are what you do." What are you doing? Can it be said that you are _actively_ seeking the presence of God in your life? If the awe or stunning greatness of God has been lost in your life (or your church), how can it be restored? But before you can consider restoring it, you have to want it! If you don't really want it then you should examine your spiritual condition and relationship to God.

(a) Do you come to worship expecting to experience God?

(b) What is your sense of God during a worship service?

(c) What is the frequency or level of recognizing your sins or sinful nature during worship?

(d) Have you ever been overcome by the greatness of God?

(e) Does God saturate your being?

(f) Is He constantly before you?

(g) Is He foremost in your thoughts?

(h) Is He the first thing you think about in the morning and the last thing at night?

11. What could you or anyone do in order to bring their lives back in tune with God or restore a relationship that has become apathetic or dulled?

WHAT DO I WANT TO REMEMBER?

Enter some notes and information that you want to remember about this lesson. It might be a Scripture verse or two, something new you learned, something you want to do, something you want to change, or just something you want to be sure to remember.

Wisdom to Action
Challenge

How can you make your worship more authentic and heartfelt this week? Choose one way to express your love, gratitude, or reverence to God more genuinely.

Lesson 9
How Should We Respond?

For thus says the One who is high and lifted up,
who inhabits eternity, whose name is Holy:
I dwell in the high and holy place, and also with
him who is of a contrite and lowly spirit,
to revive the spirit of the lowly,
and to revive the heart of the contrite.
Isaiah 57:15 ESV

The 24 elders worshipping in Revelation 4 understood how they should respond at the awesome sight of God. Not only was there praise, but there was submission. It is one thing to intellectually recognize the authority of God. It is another to actively respond, demonstrating one's own humility. The 24 elders took action to demonstrate their gratitude, love, and humility.

Jesus confirmed this when He said the disciples' love would be shown by their obedience. But life can be aggravating frust and difficult over time. It is easy to become frustrated with failures, roadblocks, and difficult people. Observe that David, a sinner just like you and me, prays *"Restore to me the joy of your salvation and grant me a willing spirit, to sustain me."* (Psalms 51:12) He needed help just like we do.

It seems clear that God is absolutely uncompromising in His requirements for worship, because worship reveals how we really feel about Him in our hearts. Isaiah 57:15 above should give us hope and guide us in the nature of our "response."

Jesus began His Sermon on the Mount with words about the poor in spirit (Matthew 5:30) and I don't think God has changed His mind since those days. I believe He expects and requires a submissive, humble, and repentant spirit. Anything less is unacceptable. If this were not the case why are the 24 worshipping elders humbling themselves and relinquishing their crowns (authority) before the throne of God?

KEY INSTRUCTIONS

REPENT
Ezekiel 18:30-32 *"Therefore I will judge you, O house of Israel, every one according to his ways, declares the Lord God. Repent and turn from all your transgressions, lest iniquity be your ruin. 31 Cast away from you all the transgressions that you have committed, and make yourselves a new heart and a new spirit! Why will you die, O house of Israel? 32 For I have no pleasure in the death of anyone, declares the Lord God; so turn, and live."* ESV

OBEDIENCE
John 14:15 *If you love me, you will keep my commandments.* ESV

HUMILITY
1 Peter 5:5 . . . *Clothe yourselves, all of you, with humility toward one another, for "God opposes the proud but gives grace to the humble."* ESV

SERVICE
Isaiah 6:8 *And I heard the voice of the Lord saying, "Whom shall I send, and who will go for us?" Then I said, "Here am I! Send me."* ESV

In a spiritual sense, humility is an internal grace of the soul that allows one to think of himself no more highly than he ought to think (Ephesians 4:1-2; Colossians 3:12-13; cf. Romans 12:3). Humility should be first directed toward God (Matthew 11:29; James 1:21). A humble spirit does not demand undue self-depreciation but rather lowliness of self-estimation and freedom from vanity. It denotes "gentleness" and "meekness" which expresses a spirit of obedience.

The person with a contrite spirit weeps over wrongdoing and expresses genuine sorrow for his own sin (Matthew 5:4; Luke 6:21; 2 Corinthians 7:10). A contrite heart is one in which natural pride and self-sufficiency have been humbled by the consciousness of sin and one's ultimate dependence on God.

WHEN PEOPLE TRULY WORSHIP, GOD SHOWS UP!

2 Chronicles 7:1, 3-4 *As soon as Solomon finished his prayer, fire came down from heaven and consumed the burnt offering and the sacrifices, and the glory of the Lord filled the temple. . . . 3 When all the people of Israel saw the fire come down and the glory of the Lord on the temple, they bowed down with their faces to the ground on the pavement and worshiped and gave thanks to the Lord, saying, "For he is good, for his steadfast love endures forever." 4 Then the king and all the people offered sacrifice before the Lord.* ESV

God's response to Solomon's prayer and the dedication of the temple in 2 Chronicles 7:1-4 underscores God's faithfulness, presence, and responsiveness to sincere worship and devotion.

What we can learn from this passage:

1. Solomon: Solomon's prayer was characterized by humility, recognition of God's faithfulness, and a plea for forgiveness and guidance for the people (2 Chronicles 6:12-42). While no human is perfect, Solomon's earnest desire to seek God's will and lead the people in righteousness likely played a significant role in His response.

2. Faithfulness: God had promised to dwell among His people in the temple if they followed His ways and obeyed His commands (2 Chronicles 7:17-18). The fire from heaven symbolized God's acceptance of Solomon's prayer and the consecration of the temple as a place of worship.

3. Grace: The people of Israel, represented by Solomon and their leaders, were seeking God's favor and forgiveness. While no one deserves God's blessings based on their own merit, God will respond to genuine repentance, humility, and faithfulness.

4. Lessons to Learn:

- God's Presence and Power: The fire from heaven demonstrated His willingness to manifest His power.
- Faithfulness to His Promises: God honors His promises and commitments. He responds to sincere prayers and acts of devotion that align with *His* will and purposes.
- Importance of Worship and Sacrifice: The act of sacrifice and worship was central to the dedication of the temple. It symbolized the people's commitment to honor and worship God.
- Spiritual Symbolism: The fire can also be seen as a symbol of purification and consecration, signifying God's cleansing of His people and the temple.

REPENT

Ezekiel 18:30-32 *"Therefore I will judge you, O house of Israel, every one according to his ways, declares the Lord God. Repent and turn from all your transgressions, lest iniquity be your ruin. 31 Cast away from you all the transgressions that you have committed, and make yourselves a new heart and a new spirit! Why will you die, O house of Israel? 32 For I have no pleasure in the death of anyone, declares the Lord God; so turn, and live."* ESV

God instructs His people to turn away from all their offenses. They are to rid themselves of all their offensive behavior. Repent or "turn away" means they are to turn from sin and turn toward God. They are to change and transform their lives.

This is the same message to the churches in Revelation 2-3 (see Revelation 2:5, 16, 22, 3:3, 19). It is also the same message to the disciples in Mark 6:12, to John The Baptist in Mt 3:2, and confirmed by Jesus in Matthew 4:17 (see also Luke 13:3-5 and

15:7). In effect this is the same message of submission we see in Revelation 4:10 by the 24 elders.

The key to submission is obedience. Both require an intentional act. John 14:15 says "If you love me, you will obey what I command." Your actions will prove what you are saying or singing in a worship service. James (2:14-26) compares faith and deeds and says <u>worship</u> by itself, if not accompanied by action, is dead. If there is no intent on our part to serve God after a "wonderful worship service" that service was probably not pleasing to God.

SUBMISSION

Ephesians 5:21-24 calls for submission. It is an expected response to a sovereign God. It means we are compliant, humble, and yielding to God's authority or will.

Ephesians 5:21-24 *Submitting to one another out of reverence for Christ. Wives and Husbands 22 Wives, submit to your own husbands, as to the Lord. 23 For the husband is the head of the wife even as Christ is the head of the church, his body, and is himself its Savior. 24 Now as the church submits to Christ, so also wives should submit in everything to their husbands.* ESV

HUMILTY

What acts or behaviors would you use to describe someone who is humble? The obvious ones are that they are not proud, and they put others needs ahead of their own. They will serve others before they take time for themselves. They typically seek to be in the background and will often avoid promotion or recognition for their service.

Obviously Jesus was an outstanding example of a humble person. He taught His disciples humility by modeling meekness when He washed their feet. When He finished washing feet He said, "I have set you an example that you should do as I have done for you." (John 13:15)

Matthew 11:28-30 . . . I am gentle and humble in heart . . .

Mark 10:45 . . . the Son of Man did not come to be served, but to serve . . .

It requires a true disciple to "know" God, and to "see the throne" in order to respond "Here I am, send me." Note what Isaiah did just before he responded "send me." (Isaiah 6:5) He admitted his guilt and his sinful nature.

Someone with a true servant's heart is one who has humbled himself before God and man, surrendered his rights, and is willing to serve the Master at any cost. This is a true worshipper!

Jesus sacrificed and suffered for you on the cross. He shed His blood so that your sins would be covered in the presence of a holy and righteous God. He humbled Himself and paid the ultimate sacrificial price out of love. What do you need to sacrifice? What do you need to give up, repent of, or change in your life? What do you need to surrender?

DISCUSSION QUESTIONS

As we complete our study on worship, how do you feel about the subject? What is your attitude toward worship? How important should it be in your life? Have your views about worship changed in the last nine weeks?

1. Have your actions or behaviors about worship changed in any way? Do you think they need to change?

2. Henry Blackaby believes the life of a worshipper often begins in private. He suggests that the foundation of worship is laid in corporate worship: the public expression of what has been going on in a private relationship with the Lord. Do you believe that it is true? Why? Why not? What is your view of public worship?

3. Has God ever shown up in some special way in a worship service you attended? If so, what happened?

4. What does Revelation 2-3 say will be given to those who are overcomers?

2:7

2:11

2:17

2:26

3:5

3:12

3:21

5. In reflecting over the past nine lessons, what do you think are your top three priorities for your personal worship?

1)

2)

3)

6. What are the things we should do in our corporate worship?

7. In Malachi 3:10 God says test me . . . "put me to the test, says the Lord of hosts!"(ESV) If we accepted God's challenge in regard to worship, what might we do? Be specific.

WHAT DO I WANT TO REMEMBER?

Enter some notes and information that you want to remember about this lesson. It might be a Scripture verse or two, something new you learned, something you want to do, something you want to change, or just something you want to be sure to remember.

Wisdom to Action
Challenge

What aspect of God's character or truth from His Word can you meditate on this week to deepen your worship? How will you allow this truth to shape your expressions of worship?

Appendix A
Worship Study Summary

The following are questions you many want to think about, consider, meditate on, or pray about as you conclude this study. If you are in a study group, think about which questions your group might help you answer.

1. FOCUS: Is the Lord Jesus Christ my primary focus, the number one priority of my life?

    a. Is my focus on Christ? (Matthew 12:28-30).
    b. Is He constantly in mind? Is He foremost in my thoughts?

2. PREPARED: Do I come to worship prepared (with clean hands and a pure heart)? (Psalm 24:3-4)

    a. Am I repentant and forgiven; do I come to worship free from sin?
    b. Have I read or studied the scripture, and prepared my life for worship in prayer?

3. HEART: Am I coming with the right heart attitude?

    a. Is my worship external and superficial or is it internal – coming from my heart?
    b. Do I come to worship humble and with a contrite heart (surrendered)?
    c. Am I motivated by my love of Jesus and His sacrifice – do I have a passion for the Christ?
    d. The early saints bowed down in worship to God and the Lord Jesus – is my heart bowed down?

4. LIVING SACRIFICE - Life: (Romans 12:1)

a. Have I submitted my life to Christ? Have I laid my crowns at His feet?
b. Am I bringing the proper spiritual offerings or spiritual sacrifices: Faith (Philippians 2:17); Material Gifts (Philippians 4:18); Life (Romans 12:1); Praise (Hebrews 13:15).
c. God is not fooled by words. Is there evidence in my life of true obedience?

5. SPIRIT and TRUTH:

a. Do I allow the Spirit to lead, teach, and guide me in worship and in my life?
b. Is my worship and life rooted and cleansed by His Word?
c. Am I honoring God in worship? Is my worship consistent with His desires?
d. Have I substituted rites, ceremonies, or activity for true heartfelt worship?

6. LIVING STONE – Church: Am I an active and contributing part of the church fellowship?

a. Do I contribute to the unity of the church? Is my focus on Christ or others rather than on self?
b. Is my commitment complete, or am I only partially committed?

7. ENCOUNTER: Am I coming I anticipation, expecting to encounter God?

a. Am I experiencing the fire (power) of God? Do I have a: sense of His glory, a conviction of sin, a desire to repent, or a power in my ministry?
b. Am I doing anything that would help me experience the presence of God (spiritual disciplines)?

8. SABBATH: Am I honoring and keeping the "Sabbath" (Lord's Day) holy?

  a. Am I participating in corporate worship?
  b. Am I honoring God on my day of worship and rest?

9. UNACCEPTABLE:

  a. Is my worship ignorant, improper, inferior, in vain, false, or without repentance in any way?
  b. Am I doing anything in worship that is unacceptable to God: disrespect; unclean; not from heart; external or superficial; conflict with the Word; not focused on Christ?

Appendix B
Prayer of Preparation for Worship

ATONEMENT
Lord Jesus, thank you for paying my sin debt and allowing me to have a right standing before you and the Father. Your blood has covered my sin making me acceptable in Your sight.

CONFESSION
Lord, forgive me for the sin in my life. I specifically ask forgiveness for: _____.
Search my heart and make known to me any offense for which I should seek Your forgiveness.

WORD
Lord, cleanse me through Your Word. Allow me knowledge and understanding that I may know You and follow Your ways. Create in me a heart that is guided by the truth of Your Word.

LIGHT
Lord, make my light shine before men. Allow other to see You in me. Help me to be a "standing stone" that points to you. Make my life reflect You so that others may also know the hope and life that only You provide.

OFFERING
Lord, my offering today is my life. My desire is to please you in everything I do. I praise you for who you are and the mighty works of Your hands. You are worthy of my praise. Please accept my offering of praise, adoration, love, and obedience as an act of worship. May my offering be acceptable in Your sight.

IN SPIRIT
Lord, I desire to worship in spirit and in truth. I want to be a true worshipper. Teach me Your ways. Fill me with your Spirit that I may be obedient to your calling on my life. Help me hear Your voice today. I want to encounter You in a special way today – through the music, preaching, teaching, prayer, and the reading of Your Word. I come in expectancy wanting meet You. AMEN!

Transformation Road Map

Primary Takeaways

1: True worship stems from a heartfelt delight in God, characterized by gratitude, humility, and a willingness to surrender everything to Him. This delight should be reflected in both our inward attitudes and outward actions, causing us to prioritize God above all else and express that priority through authentic worship.

2: Acceptable worship requires a heart transformed by God's Word. Worship is rooted in a true understanding of His glory rather than empty rituals or mere emotionalism. Our faith walk should fuel heartfelt worship that reflects His character and truth to the outside world.

3: Our sin is covered once and for all be the completed work of Christ. Our grateful response is that that we worship an amazing worthy God, presenting our lives as a living sacrifice which is now holy and acceptable to God!

4: We must intentionally set aside time to rest, reflect on God's goodness, and corporately worship with fellow believers. This act of devotion honors God and allows for a deeper understanding and enjoyment of His person and presence.

5: God still requires a sacrifice, but today that is in the form of offering our entire life as a living sacrifice, surrendering our desires, and conforming to His will. This devotion is comes from a transformed heart and mind that represents our spiritual act of worship.

6: God must be the central focus in our lives! This requires exclusive devotion, prompting a transformation of the heart that results in worship rooted in genuine love and holiness.

7: Our worship should involve engaging with God authentically, allowing His Word to transform our hearts and minds. This should result in heartfelt expressions of love, gratitude, and reverence that reflect His glory. Worship is a natural outflow of a life centered on Him.

8: Authentic worship stems from a heart transformed by biblical truth. It expresses genuine gratitude and awe for God's greatness and prioritizes seeking a deeper understanding of Him through His Word. Knowledge of God should fuel heartfelt worship that reflects His character and brings Him glory.

What are you being called to do next?

Leader Guide

This Guide is designed to give a leader answers and additional information to effectively lead a discussion of each lesson in this book.

Tips For Leading

We recommend that you begin a group discussion by reading an appropriate Scripture. It may be one that you will cover in the material or another related passage you have chosen. This will do several things:

- Allow time for everyone to get settled.
- Remind everyone of the subject and bring their minds to a common focus.
- Provide a transition from the previous activity.

Additional ice-breakers are usually not necessary, but if your group is new or members don't know each other well, you could have someone give their testimony/story at the beginning of each week. If you sense that the group needs additional focus before you begin with the discussion, conduct a short discussion about the themes of the lesson or ask about the meaning of a particular term associated with the lesson.

Goals

The discussion should center around the questions in the lesson. But remember that each person in your group has different goals and is at a different place in his or her Christian walk. Jesus may be an old friend to some but a new acquaintance to others. The dynamic of the group will vary depending on the nature of the participants.

Your goal as the Leader should be to foster understanding and familiarity with Scripture. For new believers or participants who are not comfortable with the Bible, your goal should be to help them get over that hurdle and begin to seek knowledge and understanding from His Word.

More mature participants will probably dig deeper to find personal meaning and understanding. They may particularly desire to discuss application questions and issues.

Prayer

Unless you have an outstanding person of prayer in your group, you as the leader should wrap up your discussion time with prayer that specifically reflects the discussion and the themes, purpose, and focus of the lesson.

Answers

Chapter 1 Delight in Worship

MEDITATION

LEADER: You may want to lead a special prayer time for your group.

Preparation: SING: *I love you Lord, and I lift my voice, to worship You, Oh, my soul – rejoice. Take joy my King, in what You hear, may it be a sweet, sweet song in Your ear.*

Prayer topics:

1 Help me (our church) understand the meaning of true worship.

2 Open my heart so the message can get from the mind to the heart.

3 Identify to me those things I do in worship (we do as a church) that are unacceptable to God.

4 Help me focus on God during worship – blot out world around me so my focus is only on God.

5 Give me a new attitude and excitement about worship.

6 Allow me to experience the greatness of God.

7 Make the Lord Jesus Christ the central focus of my life and my worship.

8 Praise.

DELIGHT YOURSELF

LEADER: You may want to ask the following questions in discussing this topic:

Q. Do you "delight" in the Lord? Why? Why not?

Q. What do you think it means to delight in God/Jesus?

Ps 37:4   the desires of your heart

Ps 35:9   salvation

Ps 112:1   His commands

Isa 11:3   fear of the Lord

Isa 58:13   keep your feet from breaking the Sabbath

Isa 61:10   clothed me with salvation and a robe of righteousness

Isaiah 58:2 righteous judgments

James 4:8 He will come near to you.

God delights in:

Ro 12:1-2 _____offering my life as a spiritual sacrifice

Ro 14:17-18 _____righteousness, peace, joy in the Holy Spirit

Php 4:18 _____offerings, tithes, gifts

1 Tim 5:4 _____caring for family
Heb 13:29-21 _____His will working in us

Q1. How do you react to the above?
Overwhelmed by the thought that I am a child of God, a member of the family of God, a co-heir with Christ!
Q2.
LEADER: Remember our definition is: *The rituals, ceremonies, and activities by which we express reverent devotion, homage, and allegiance to God; acknowledgment of God, of His nature, attributes, ways and claims, whether by the outgoing of the heart in praise and thanksgiving or by deeds done in such acknowledgment.*
Q3.
Ans: Reverence/submission/homage.
HOMAGE: Reverential regard, respect, acts that attest to the worth/influence/position of another
NOTE: The word "worship" appears with bow/bowed in same verse 32 times throughout Scripture.
LEADER: You might read the following to group after the discussion:
In the Old Testament there are 2 words predominantly used for "worship." One is related to our work or service, which is a form of worship. The other is *shachah* which means to <u>prostrate oneself</u>, to bow down, to stoop before. In the New Testament the primary word used is *proskuneo* and it means essentially the same thing (to crouch, to prostrate oneself in homage, to revere and adore, with the added picture of kissing the hand). In the Old Testament we see many examples of people bowing in worship. In the New Testament this bowing is clearly the *bowing of one's heart before God.*
Q4.
LEADER: After the discussion read from Exodus 20:2ff.
2 "I am the LORD your God . . ."
3 "You shall have no other gods before me."
4 "You shall not make for yourself an idol in the form of anything . . ."
5 You shall not bow down to them or worship them; for I, the LORD your God, am a jealous God . . ."
7 "You shall not misuse the name of the LORD your God . . ."
8 "Remember the Sabbath day by keeping it holy. . . ."
Mark 12:29-30 *"The most important one," answered Jesus, "is this: 'Hear, O Israel, the Lord our God, the Lord is one. 30 Love the Lord your God with all your heart and with all your soul and with all your mind and with all your strength."* NIV
CONCLUSION: Worship should be at the top of our priority list.
LEADER: Then ask, "Now, does anyone believe the most important issue is something other than who we worship?"
Q5.
No! Granted people are free to ascribe worth to anyone or anything – but God is very clear: there is only <u>one</u> God, and He alone is to be worshipped, and, in the way <u>He</u> prescribes!
Q6.

24:3. To Jerusalem to worship at the temple.

24:4. Clean hands and pure heart!

Lifting your soul to what is false and not swearing deceitfully is describing what it means to have clean hands and a pure heart.

Q7.

LEADER: [It may not be too much of a stretch to say that many people know God by what He has done for them rather than for who He is. We must worship God for who He is, not just for what He has done.]

In the OT the people knew God by the Names of God; When God passed by Moses, what did Moses see and report: the attributes of God.

What has God disclosed about Himself, that we can learn and understand?

God has indeed through revelation declared certain things to be true about Himself – the attributes of God – things that can rightly or correctly be ascribed to God. We must acknowledge that the number of attributes may be limitless, but as an example we could list the following characteristics of God: Creator – Sustainer; Eternal; Faithful; Forgiving; Good; Grace; Holy; Immutable – unchanging; Jealous; Judge; Just; King; Love; Mercy – compassion; Omnipotent – mighty; Omniscient – all knowing; Omnipresent; One; Perfect; Provider; Supreme – sovereign; Trinity – 3 in 1; True; Wise; Wrathful; a Consuming Fire; Perfect; Righteous; Patient; Infinitude (knows no limit or bounds).

Q8.

His Word. Paul, for example, describes God in 1 Timothy 1:17 *Now to the King eternal, immortal, invisible, the only God, be honor and glory for ever and ever. Amen.* NIV

Q9.

9a.

(1) **The Lion of Judah**

See Gen 49:9-10...the Messiah would come from the line of Judah

(2) **The Root of David**

In Jesus day He was called the "son of David" because he was a direct ancestor of King David...root seems to imply both father and son. In His deity Jesus was before David and in His humanity He was in the ancestry of David.

(3) **The Lamb that was slain**

He is worthy to open the scroll in Rev 5 because of His sacrifice for sin.

NOTE: He came first as a Lamb to die for us and will return as a Lion to rule the earth.

9b.

Everyone...every creature would include animals.

Revelation 5:13 Then I heard <u>every creature</u> in heaven and on earth and under the earth and on the sea, and all that is in them, singing: "To him who sits on the throne and to the Lamb be praise and honor and glory and power, for ever and ever!" NIV

Q10. n/a

Lesson 2 What is Acceptable Worship?

Q1.

1. acceptably

2. priest, priest

3. Christ
4. sin
5. clean hands and pure heart
6. life
7. message of (light) and (life) to me
8. Word
9. heart
10. prayer
Q2.
HEART: 1) The inner self, 2) Your true character, 3) The center of man's being, 4) The center of man's rational nature, 5) The seat of true personality, 6) The source of all that is good and evil in man, 7) The seat of conscience, and 8) It is the center of the entire man, the very origin of life's impulse.

DISCUSSION QUESTIONS

1. What it means to worship: Our definition is on the first page of the lesson. Generally, someone might say, "Worship is the act of reverently honoring and adoring God. It involves expressing love, devotion, and respect towards God through various forms such as prayer, singing, reading Scripture, hearing God's Word taught, and living a life that reflects His glory."

2. The most important thing to do in worship: The most important thing in worship is to focus on God with a sincere heart. This includes offering genuine praise and thanksgiving, confessing sins, listening to God's Word with openness, and responding obediently to His leading.

3. Why Christian congregations sing and biblical requirement: Singing in Christian congregations is a common form of worship found throughout the Bible, including the Psalms (Psalm 100:1-2; Psalm 95:1-2). It allows believers to collectively express praise, unity, and joy in God's presence. While singing is not explicitly commanded as the sole form of worship, it is a powerful means of communal worship and spiritual expression.

4. Importance of having your heart engaged in worship: We defined the "heart" at the end of our lesson. Having one's heart engaged in worship is crucial because it reflects the sincerity and authenticity of our worship. Jesus emphasized that true worshipers worship in spirit and in truth (John 4:23-24), indicating that genuine worship involves both heartfelt devotion and alignment with God's revealed truth. Without genuine engagement of the heart, worship can become ritualistic or superficial.

5. Appropriate, expected, or desired responses in worship: In a worship service, the desired responses include reverence, humility, gratitude, and a readiness to receive God's Word. Worship involves responding to God's presence and truth with obedience, surrender, and a desire to glorify Him in all aspects of life.

Lesson 3 Old Testament Worship and the Tabernacle
Q1.
God gave instructions on how it was to be done – He was very specific and detailed. Thus, there must be very good and meaningful reasons for doing it just as God commanded.
Q2.
Manifest means: readily perceived by the senses; recognized; to be evident.

Jn 1:14; in Jesus
1 Cor 6:19-20); us
Q3.
We are! 1 Peter 2:9 *But you are a chosen race, a royal priesthood, a holy nation, a people for his own possession, that you may proclaim the excellencies of him who called you out of darkness into his marvelous light.* ESV
Q4.
I do not need an intermediary – I can communicate directly with God. But just as the job of the priest was to be an intermediary, I could serve that function by introducing others to God ... which was one of the ultimate purposes of Israel. I should feel very fortunate and humble. I am in this position only by the grace of God.
LEADER: The key point to understand in this section is that we are now the priests and thus fulfill the same function of the OT priest.
Q5.
If we are going to worship God it <u>must</u> be done through Christ, since He is the <u>only access</u> to the Father.
Q6.
The individual brought the offering (you). He presented it at the entrance, then, placed his hand on the head of the animal (in order to receive atonement). He was to be the one to kill the sacrifice (not the priest) before the LORD.
Q7.
First, we need to be free of sin before we can go any farther.
NOTE: This may be <u>THE</u> really important fact we need to understand! We must deal with our sin before we can truly worship.
Q8.
He covered our sins. We are made holy – once for all time.
Q9.
We must be <u>clean</u>! We must do it so it is pleasing to Him, not necessarily to us. For the Old Testament priest who did not follow God's instructions, the penalty was death, so it was <u>important</u>!
Q10.
We are to confess our sins....if we do He will forgive us and purify us. Purify us for what: worship!
Q11.
We must accept Christ (only believers can worship); be holy; be forgiven for our sins (cleansed); be pure.
Q12.
Given that God is very particular about how we worship, what we do, and the condition of our hearts and minds, it is ludicrous to think He would not insist on this requirement.
Q13.
We must be rooted in the Word.
Q14.
The priests ate the bread, but in the new covenant, we are priests, therefore, we must be sustained by the Word of God in our worship and in our life.
Q15.
Christ is the <u>only</u> source of the "light of life" for mankind.

Q16.

Purpose: On the Day of Atonement the incense was burned to create smoke to conceal the atonement cover (mercy seat) when the priest went behind the curtain.

Q17.

The priest would die if he did not follow instructions, showing that God is <u>very</u> particular about how we worship. God is holy.

Discussion Questions:

1.

(a) Maybe worship is more than I supposed; (b) worship is not as simple as I want to make it.

2.

TRICK QUESTION: God wants our <u>best!</u>

We need to come to worship for the right reasons.

Out of a spirit of love, which is a decision based on who He is and what He has done, not out of some sense of obligation, rule, or requirement.

We worship out of love – not duty, out of a desire to be obedient. Because He is worthy!

3A.

Make ourselves clean; stop evil; stop doing wrong; seek justice; encourage the oppressed; defend fatherless; care for widows.

3B.

More specific about our actual behavior.

3C.

Their hearts were not in it. Even here we see the real issue is not the burnt offerings, it is an issue of the heart.

4.

Love of God.

5.

YES – But it's true and heart-felt obedience.

NO – Then what is?

If not obedience, then we can choose to worship any way we want and that is not consistent with all God's instructions concerning worship.

Another possible answer is: God.

Abraham: obeyed, so his son was spared. David was a man after God's heart because God knew He would obey.

LEADER: Let me ask this: "Do you think you can worship if you're living a life of disobedience? Why? Why not?

6. n/a

7. n/a

8. n/a

Lesson 4 the Sabbath

Q1.

WORK: stores and malls.

RECREATION/PLEASURE: boats, cars . . .

PRIORITY: As a nation we have lost our focus on God on Sunday.

Q2.

Compromise the absolute truth of the Gospel; accept sin; prefer to offend God rather than people on Sunday morning.

Q3.

Many believe the church will pay a high price with God (spiritual disaster) because God will withdraw his presence, power, and blessing.

He may even impose discipline and judgment. Why? Because the Sabbath is serious to God.

Q4.

"Disdained" means contempt; often considered unworthy or inferior.

Modern Day: We work, we shop, we do not rest, and we do not focus on God.

Most of us give God one hour on Sunday, versus all day.

Q5.

This issue about keeping the Sabbath is not a matter of legalism, but about respect and honoring God. It is God's desire for us to corporately worship Him and that did not change when Jesus arrived on the scene.

Q6. n/a

Q7.

LEADER: You may want to stop and pray about this subject.

DISCUSSION QUESTIONS

LEADER: Before you begin you might start with a broad general question: "Does anyone have any questions or concerns about the history and meaning of the Jewish Sabbath?"

1. n/a

2.

Observe the Sabbath (as a sign).

It is to be holy.

No work – a day of rest.

It is a day for celebrating.

The penalty for desecration is death (desecration = being profane, disrespectful, and irreverent.)

3.

Set apart, different, special, a focus on God.

LEADER NOTE: the meaning here is not "set apart" so much as: "clean" – "consecrated" – "dedicated" – "sanctified"

The objective is to be ceremonially or morally clean.

The intent and reason for the Sabbath is to be totally focused on God. That is how we make it holy!

4.

It's His day; do only things that honor Him; set worldly things aside.

The focus should be on God, a time when God could speak to us!

5.

Lord:	Bow down in submission.
Creator:	Praise Him.
Redeemer:	Be thankful.

6.

IF: You (1) consider the day a delight and honor it; and (2) obey and not do your own thing.

THEN: Find joy in the Lord and His physical rewards (bountiful land).

Lesson 5 God Requires a Sacrifice!

1.

It is to be discovered; it will prove to be good, acceptable, and perfect.

It requires a sacrifice – placing ourselves on the altar and submitting to God.

The purpose is knowing God's will for our lives.

2.

Our values, commitments, pleasures, and particularly what we tolerate and accept.

3.

Through (1) service, (2) study, and (3) worship.

- Complete; offer your bodies; all we are; all we do; no partial commitment.
- Living; Jesus is the first and last; die to self and live for God. It is to be continuous.
- Holy and pleasing to God; have clean hands and pure heart (Ps 24:3-4). They may imply a continuous life of confession and repentance.
- Acceptable: do not conform to the world.
- Transformed by the renewing of your mind: change your character, behavior, and heart.

4.

Living.

Holy.

Acceptable: do not conform to the world.

Transformed by the renewing of your mind.

Complete: offer our bodies (life).

5. n/a

DISCUSSION QUESTIONS: General

1.

1) The heart is right; no anger; do what is right.

2) God did not look with favor on Cain or his offerings and Cain reacted in anger.

3) God knew Cain's heart, attitude, and motivations were not right.

2.

Why not! There is *life in the blood*. That is His requirement and He is God.

Leviticus 17:11 *For the life of the flesh is in the blood, and I have given it for you on the altar to make atonement for your souls, for it is the blood that makes atonement by the life.* ESV

UNDERSTAND: My debt had to be covered by blood, by a sacrificial Lamb without blemish. Jesus is that perfect Lamb. Thus, God has personally paid my sin debt and He did it once for all. But I must come in saving faith, believing.

3.

It means we have internalized it.

4.

Rid ourselves of sin. We must come clean.

5.

Philippians 2:17	Faith
Philippians 4:18	Material gifts
Romans 12:1	Lives (bodies)

Hebrews 13:15   Praise
Romans 15:16   Gentiles
6.
Our hearts and lives prepared . . . TO WORSHIP.
7.
We must rid ourselves of malice, and all deceit, etc.
This is confirmed by Ps 24:3-4 *Who may ascend the hill of the LORD? Who may stand in his holy place? 4 He who has clean hands and a pure heart, who does not lift up his soul to an idol or swear by what is false.*
8.
God wants my walk to be blameless and righteous. I should speak truth, not slander, and do what is right.
LEADER: You might ask, "BUT, if sinful man cannot meet these requirements, then what must we do to come acceptably before a holy God?" Ans: Confess; repent; ask for forgiveness.
9.
Some worship and behavior is unacceptable. God will hide from me and reject my worship, prayer, deeds.
     Q. Not that I can find in Scripture!
10.

Worship God Accepts	Worship God Rejects
from the heart	rote activity – mechanical
heart right, no anger	offensive way in heart
doing what is right; holy; blameless	sinful behavior
repentant heart	no repentance
focus on Christ	focus on self, people, music
full commitment	partial commitment

11.
(1) obligation, (2) habit, (3) what you will get, or hope to get (4) to worship King Jesus!

Lesson 6 God is Central!
Q1.
If we have idols or other gods in our life we are rejecting the one true God. We can't claim real allegiance to the Lord if we worship other gods. The question then becomes, "If we have other gods in our life, where do we stand with the one true God?"
Q2. n/a
Q3.
Matthew 6:33 *But seek first his kingdom and his righteousness, and all these things will be given to you as well.* NIV
Q4a.
Small group, accountability partner, or the power of Holy Spirit.
Q4b. n/a
Q5.
1 John 5:20   To know Christ means we must know God.
1 John 2:3   Obey.
1 John 2:6   Walk as Jesus did.
1 John 4:21   Love God!

Q6 n/a
Q7.
a. ___ Avoid Punishment
b. ___Freedom
c. ___Attain resurrection
Exercise
Here are possible responses for someone giving reasons they know Jesus as their personal Lord and Savior:

1. **Personal Experience of Transformation:** They may talk about how their life has been changed by encountering Jesus, such as experiencing forgiveness, peace, joy, or having a sense of purpose.
2. **Prayer Life:** They might discuss their ongoing communication with God in prayer and examples of answered prayer.
3. **Biblical Knowledge and Understanding:** They may mention their knowledge of Scripture and how it has deepened their understanding of who Jesus is and what He has done for them.
4. **Fruit of the Spirit:** They might point to the evidence of spiritual fruit in their lives—love, joy, peace, patience, kindness, goodness, faithfulness, gentleness, and self-control (Galatians 5:22-23).
5. **Community and Fellowship:** They may talk about their involvement in a Christian community, where they experience mutual encouragement, support, and growth in their faith.
6. **Changed Priorities and Values:** They might discuss how their priorities and values have shifted as a result of following Jesus, focusing more on eternal things rather than worldly pursuits.
7. **Witnessing:** They may mention their desire or actions to share their faith with others and to live as a witness for Christ in their daily life.
8. **Peace in Trials:** They might share how their faith in Jesus has given them peace and strength during difficult times and trials.
9. **Holy Spirit's Guidance:** They may talk about how they rely on the Holy Spirit for guidance, wisdom, and discernment in their life.
10. **Continual Growth and Learning:** They might discuss their ongoing journey of spiritual growth, learning more about God and deepening their relationship with Him over time.
11. **Experience of Grace and Mercy:** They may share personal stories of experiencing God's grace, forgiveness, and mercy in their life.
12. **Conviction and Assurance:** They might talk about the inner assurance and conviction they have that Jesus is real and alive, based on their personal encounters with Him.
13. **Acts of Service and Compassion:** They perform acts of service and compassion towards others as expressions of their love for Jesus and desire to follow His example.
14. **Peace in Decision-Making:** They might discuss how they experience peace in their decisions when they align them with God's will.
15. **Hope for Eternity:** They may express their assurance of eternal life with God through Jesus Christ, based on His promises in Scripture.

Q8.
YES – I want to be holy; imitate Him
NO – Probably don't want to know Him
Q9. n/a
Q10. n/a
Q11.
You may be more concerned about your comfort, your thoughts, your priorities, or your problems. God may not be at the top of your conscious list.
LEADER: Ask: "If that's true, how do you suspect God is reacting to your disinterested or cavalier attitude?"
Q12. n/a
Q13.

Verse	What do
1:	exalt; praise His name forever (worship)
2:	extol; praise every day
4:	commend His works to one another; tell of His mighty acts
5:	speak of His splendor/majesty; meditate on His works (study)
6:	tell of God's power – in His works; proclaim His great deeds
7:	celebrate God's goodness; sing of His righteousness (worship)
10:	praise God, extol God
11:	tell of glory of God's Kingdom; speak of God's might (testify)
18:	call on God in truth (prayer)
19:	fear God ("fear")
20:	love Him (love)
21:	speak in praise; praise forever (worship)

Lesson 7 Worship in Spirit and Truth
Q1.
Veil will be torn; destruction of temple in 70 AD; sacrifices will not be possible without the temple. This foretells or warns of a change in worship and how we should approach God.
Q2.
Zeph 3:14 Sing, shout, be glad
Ps 37:4   Delight in God -> He will give the desires of your heart
Ps 73:25 We are desired by God and in heaven together.
Q3.
a. Experience great ANTICIPATION in approaching Sunday morning worship.
b. Experience great PLEASURE in giving tithes and offerings.
c. Experience great SATISFACTION in serving others, helping the needy, etc.
d. Experience significant INTIMACY in personal times of prayer and worship.
Q4.
Worship in SPIRIT: CHACTERISTICS:

1) born of the Spirit	John 3:6-7
2) yield to His control	Eph 5:8
3) respond with contrite repentant hearts	Isa 66:2
4) focus on God	Ps 86:11
5) glory in Christ	Php 3:3
6) put no confidence in the flesh	Php 3:3

Q5. n/a
Q6.
Worship may occur anywhere your spirit connects with God!
Q7.
Do not let emotions carry you away from God. Focus on Him exclusively.
Dangers: 1) music, 2) people, 3) worldly cares, 4) worldly success.
DISCUSSION QUESTIONS
1. n/a
2.
a. Music: more entertainment than induce worship.
b. People: sexually suggestive clothing; harsh or loud talking.
c. Worldly cares, concerns, problems, or suffering.
d. Apathy or a wandering mind – no ability to focus.
e. No conviction of sin.
f.   Lack of focus on Jesus or God's Word.
LEADER: You might ask, "How might these distractions be minimized?"
3.
We need to be sanctified, made holy, and consecrated by God's Word.
4.
 Did you pray about the service in some way?
Did you read the sermon Scripture before Sunday?
Did you meditate over the issue of pleasing God in worship?
What did you do to come before a holy God?
5.
By the Spirit we glory in Christ.
God is Spirit [invisible, divine, and life-giving].
God is not confined to things, idol worship is repugnant.
He is not confined to places. He cannot be limited to the Temple.
Our gifts must be gifts of the spirit (love, obedience, devotion, etc.).
Animal sacrifices are inadequate.
Man's spirit is what will last and it is the spirit that attains intimacy with God.
True worship is when man's spirit meets or engages with God.
Worship no longer took place in Jerusalem or Mt. Gerizim.
The spirit of truth is (1) God centered, (2) enabled by Holy Spirit, and (3) conforming to the Word.
6.
LEADER: You might ask, "Is it possible that your worship is ever 'in vain'?"
In "vain" would mean it is meaningless or of no value. Are you uncomfortable thinking that your worship might be in vain?

Lesson 8 Worship in Heaven
DISCUSSION QUESTIONS
1.
We will worship. Worship will be a major function. Everyone worships, including leaders. It is constant.
2.
He is worthy; He is God; Creator.
3.

SURRENDER. Laying their crowns at His feet is demonstrating humble surrender and submission. These people are important: They sit on thrones and have gold crowns.

SUBMISSION: Condition of being compliant, humble, yielding to another's authority or will; to be subject to.

FALL DOWN: To lay prone or flat in humility was a physical position indicating yielding.

4.

In every case the elders are described as falling down. They clearly feel the need to humble themselves. Such humility could be displayed in any number of ways – here it is falling down.

5.

People follow leaders.

6.

It requires a heart posture of humility, trust, and obedience, recognizing God's sovereignty and goodness in all circumstances. We must surrender in order to experience His peace, purpose, and transformative power in our lives. Here are ways we can respond today:

a) **Acknowledge and affirm God's supreme authority over our lives.** God is the rightful ruler and authority over all aspects of our existence.

b) **Cultivate an attitude of humility and submission in our daily lives.** This involves yielding our will and desires to God, trusting His wisdom and guidance in all our decisions.

c) **Surrender involves offering our talents, abilities, and achievements to God for His glory.** Recognize that all our skills and successes are gifts from Him and should be used for His purposes.

d) **Letting go of control.** Trusting God's sovereignty allows us to release anxiety and rely on His provision.

e) **Obedience involves aligning our lives with the teachings and principles found in God's Word.** Obedience demonstrates our trust in His goodness and faithfulness.

f) **Develop a habit of surrendering daily in prayer.** Prayer becomes a dialogue of surrender as we seek His will and guidance.

g) **Prioritize God's kingdom and His righteousness above personal ambitions and worldly pursuits** (Matthew 6:33). Surrendering our priorities to God's agenda ensures we are aligned with His purposes.

7.

ESV Worship Him

NKJV Serve Him

8.

Learn and actively participate in worship.

Serve in ministry. Practice the "one anothers."

Why? So we are good at it when we get to Heaven.

9.

1) Bring an offering (sacrificial? – yes probably).

2) Come into His courts (Temple).

3) Worship in His holiness (what you do at Temple – now the church).
4) Tremble before Him (natural reaction to who He is and what He has done).
5) Say… (speak, sing praise)….Celebrate …. Not all to be serious!
10. n/a
11.
Ask for help!

Lesson 9 How Should We Respond?
DISCUSSION QUESTIONS
1. n/a
2. n/a
3. n/a
4.

2:7	the right to eat from the tree of life in paradise
2:11	not be hurt by the second death
2:17	will receive the hidden manna; white stone with new name
2:26	authority over the nations; morning star
3:5	dressed in white; in book of life; acknowledge me before Father
3:12	pillar in Temple; write my name of God + city of God + Jesus' name
3:21	right to sit with Jesus on His throne

LEADER: Ask, "How do you react to all this?" Ans: Let's CELEBRATE!
5.
LEADER: You may have answers like:
- Choose to live a lifestyle of worship.
- Anticipate encounters with God.
- Approach Scripture in an attitude of worship.
- Pray ahead of time.
- Seek the enabling of the Holy Spirit.
- Seek to know God – know His voice.
- Commitment to obedience.

6.
- Treat fellowship with the "church" as a way of life. One of those activities is attending worship services regularly.
- The NT says not to forsake meeting together – be present.
- Actively seek the presence of God. Focus on the Divine.

7. n/a

END

Free PDF
MAKE WISE DECISIONS

[Get the ebook version for 99 cents]

Consequences Shape Lives.

This book discusses the nature of decisions and explores eight essential questions to make better decisions.

You are a few decisions away from transforming your life. You can make better decisions! This resource has sections on what makes a poor decision, questions to ask yourself, traps to avoid, short and sweet decisions, the wise decision framework, and twenty ways to be wise. It also has a handy decision-making checklist. (12 pages)

Free PDF: https://getwisdompublishing.com/resource-registration/

Kindle ebook for 99 cents: https://www.amazon.com/dp/B0FG8NC53J

Ebook

Free PDF

Ten Steps to Wise Choices

Timeless Wisdom. Practical Tools. Lasting Impact.

Free PDF
Life Improvement Principles

[Get the ebook version for 99 cents]

You can live your best life!

Welcome to a journey of discovery! In case you have forgotten, your actions have consequences. Unlock your potential! This book (60+ pages) provides the overview of all our strategies and wisdom principles to live your best life. You *can* transform your life! Get your wisdom-based roadmap to a better life and unlock all the possibilities for growth and success.

Free PDF: https://getwisdompublishing.com/resource-registration/

Kindle ebook for 99 cents:
https://www.amazon.com/dp/B0FG883KZM

Ebook

Free PDF

Make it your life goal to be the best you can be!

Discover Wisdom and live the life you deserve.

What Next?
Continue Your Journey

Continue Study in the *Jesus Follower* Series
The Jesus Follower Bible Study Series
https://www.amazon.com/dp/B0DHP39P5J

Be Challenged by the *OBSCURE* Series
The *OBSCURE* Bible Study Series
https://www.amazon.com/dp/B08T7TL1B1

Tackle Wisdom-Driven Life Change
Apply Biblical Wisdom to Live Your Best Life!
"Effective Life Change"
https://www.amazon.com/dp/1952359732

Know What You Should Pray
Personal Daily Prayer Guide
https://www.amazon.com/What-Should-Pray-Personal-Journal/dp/1952359260/

Decide to be the Very Best You Can Be
The Life Planning Series
https://www.amazon.com/dp/B09TH9SYC4

You Can Help:
SOCIAL MEDIA: Mention The Jesus Follower Bible Study Series on your social platforms. Include the hashtag #jesusbiblestudy so we are aware of your post.

FRIENDS: Recommend this series to your family, friends, small group, Sunday School class leaders, or your church.

REVIEW: Please give us your honest review at
https://www.amazon.com/dp/1952359600

The OBSCURE Bible Study Series

Continue your journey through the hidden
wisdom of Scripture with the OBSCURE Series.

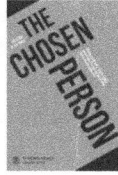

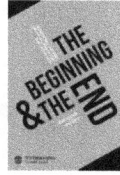

Blasphemy, Grace, Quarrels & Reconciliation: The lives of first-century disciples.
This book presents Joseph of Arimathea, Joanna, Ananias, Hymenaeus, and Cornelius (a centurion). It illustrates the nature and challenges of life as a first-century disciple.

The Beginning and the End: From creation to eternity.
This book has four lessons from Genesis and four from Revelation covering creation, rebellion, grace, worship, and eternity. God is leading us to worship in the Throne Room.

God at the Center: He is sovereign and I am not.
This book examines the virgin birth, worship, prayer, the sovereignty of God, compromise, and trust. God is at the center of all these stories. He is at the center of our lives.

Women of Courage: God did some serious business with these women.
This book examines the lives of Jael, Rizpah, the woman of Tekoa, Tabitha, Shiphrah, and Lydia. These women exhibit great courage and faithfulness. God used them in amazing ways.

The Beginning of Wisdom: Your personal character counts.
In this book we find courage, loyalty, thankfulness, love, forgiveness, and humility. Personal character counts. Decisions have consequences. Wisdom will help us stand firm in our faith.

Miracles & Rebellion: The good, the bad, and the indifferent.
God hates sin and loves to heal the faithful. The rebellion of Korah, Haman, and Alexander compare to the healing stories of Aeneas, a slave girl, and the crippled man at Lystra.

The Chosen People: There is a remnant.
This book concentrates mostly on Israel in the Old Testament, but also covers some interesting subjects as Lucifer, Michael the archangel, and Job's wife.

The Chosen Person: Keep your eyes on Jesus.
The focus is on Jesus and the superiority of Christ. We investigate Melchizedek, the disciples on the road to Emmaus, Nicodemus, and the criminal on the cross.

WEBSITE: http://getwisdompublishing.com/products/
AMAZON: www.amazon.com/author/stephenhberkey

Life Planning Series

Read these books if you want to live a better life.

The primary audience for this series is the secular self-help market, but the concepts are Christian based.

	For the spiritual seeker and those with spiritual questions. *Your Spiritual Guidebook For Questions About Religion, God, Heaven, Truth, Evil, and the Afterlife.* **https://www.amazon.com/dp/1952359473**
	Core values will drive your life. **https://www.amazon.com/dp/195235949X**

Other Titles in the Life Planning Series
CHOOSE Integrity
CHOOSE Friends Wisely
CHOOSE The Right Words
CHOOSE Good Work Habits
CHOOSE Financial Responsibility
CHOOSE A Positive Self-Image
CHOOSE Leadership
CHOOSE Love and Family
LIFE PLANNING HANDBOOK A Life Plan Is The Key To Personal Growth https://www.amazon.com/gp/product/1952359325

Go to:

https://www.amazon.com/dp/B09TH9SYC4

to get your copy.

Personal Daily Prayer Guide
Prayer Resource and Journal

This is a great resource to kick-start your prayer life!

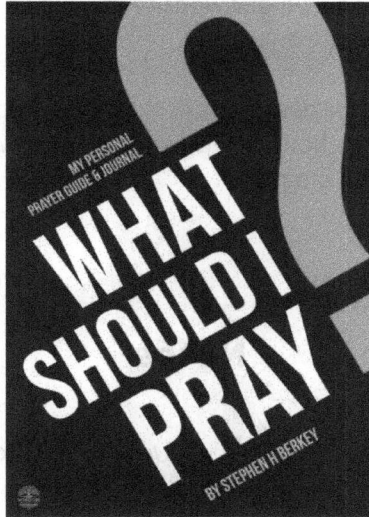

Know what to pray.
Pray based on Bible verses.
Strengthen your prayer life.
Access reference resources.
Pray with eternal implications.
Write your own prayers if desired.
Organize and focus your prayer time.
Learn what the Bible says about prayer.
Find encouragement and advice on how to pray.
Reduce frustration and distraction in your prayer time.

Get your copy today!

https://www.amazon.com/What-Should-Pray-Personal-Journal/dp/1952359260/

Acknowledgments

My wife has patiently persevered while I indulged my interest in writing. Thank you for all your help and assistance.

Our older daughter has been an invaluable resource. She has also graciously produced our website at www.getwisdompublishing.com

Our middle daughter designed the covers for most of my books, but I gave her a vacation on this Series. We are very grateful for her help, talent and creativity.

Notes

1 Lesson 3 is based on "*Living a Life of TRUE Worship*" by Kay Arthur, Published by WaterBrook, 2009, ISBN 978-0307457660.

2 John Piper, "*Let the Nations be Glad: The Supremacy of God in Missions,*" Baker Publishing Group, ISBN 9780801071249.

SPECIAL NOTE: The diagrams of the Tabernacle in Lesson 3 were provided by Barnes' Bible Charts

About the Author

Steve attended church as a child and accepted Christ when he was 10 years old. But his walk with Jesus left a lot to be desired for the next 44 years. In 1994 he "wrestled" with God for some period of months and in September of that year totally surrendered his life to Jesus.

In 1996 he was so driven to study God's Word that he attended the Indianapolis campus of Trinity Evangelical Divinity School (Chicago) to earn a Certificate of Biblical Studies. His hunger for God's Word led him to lead and write all his own Bible studies for his small group. He has been a Bible study leader for the past 25 years.

After 25 years as an actuary, and 20 years as an entrepreneur, he began his third career as an author in 2020, when he published The OBSCURE Bible Study Series. The Jesus Follower Bible Study Series was completed in early 2025. He is a member of The Church at Station Hill in Spring Hill, TN, a regional campus of Brentwood Baptist (Brentwood TN).

"Get Wisdom Publishing is dedicated to being the trusted source of wisdom-driven books that inspire growth, guide decisions, and empower readers to live with purpose and fulfillment."

Contact Us

Website: www.getwisdompublishing.com

Email: info@getwisdompublishing.com

Facebook: Get Wisdom Publishing

Author's Page:
www.amazon.com/author/stephenhberkey

Amazon's Jesus Follower Bible Study Series page:
https://www.amazon.com/dp/B0DHP39P5J

"Go beyond devotionals.
Experience biblical wisdom in action!"

GET**WISDOM**
PUBLISHING